AND GOD GAVE
THE INCREASE

AND GOD GAVE THE INCREASE

1 Corinthians 3:6–9

Stories of How the Presbyterian Church (U.S.A.)
Has Helped in the Education of Christian
Leaders around the World

June Ramage Rogers, Editor

Office of Global Education
and International Leadership Development
Worldwide Ministries Division
Presbyterian Church (U.S.A.)
Louisville, Kentucky

*A cooperative production of Mission Interpretation and Promotion, Congregational
Ministries Division, and the Office of Global Education and International Leadership and
Development, Worldwide Ministries Division, Ministries of the General Assembly Council,
Presbyterian Church (U.S.A.)*

PDS 74-320-98-001

PRINTED IN THE UNITED STATES OF AMERICA

"*I planted, Apollos watered, but God gave the increase. So neither the one who plants nor the one who waters is anything but only God who gives the increase. The one who plants and the one who waters have a common purpose, and each will receive wages according to the labor of each. For we are God's servants, working together; you are God's garden.*"

(1 Cor. 3:6–9)

TABLE OF CONTENTS

ACKNOWLEDGEMENTS

This story could not have been told without the encouragement and assistance of many friends and colleagues. Hundreds of phone calls and faxes from authors and scholars all over the world were required to secure the information needed to complete this brief history. Early conversations with Margaret Flory, Alan Hamilton, Robert Lodwick, and Haydn White, former staff of the Leadership Development Program in its many configurations, were seminal. But special thanks must go to the following persons:

To Marian McClure, who provided me with the opportunity to celebrate the Year with Education by lifting up this remarkable program of leadership development, and whose "stars project" led the way;

To the Leadership Development Scholars themselves and their inspirational lives of creative and faithful service;

To the authors, who took on the writing task as a labor of love and who met short deadlines with equanimity and patience;

To my colleagues in the Office of Global Education:

> to Jenny Stoner, whose enthusiasm and early editing made it all seem possible;
> to Roula Alkhouri, whose excitement about this history was contagious;
> to Ruth Ann Gill, whose eyes lit up as each step was completed;
> to Joel Weible, who cheerfully mailed out hundreds of questionnaires;
> to David Maxwell, whose appreciation of the stories as they appeared was an inspiration; and
> to Bill Rogers, whose love and support were essential;

To Sandra Moak Sorem and Maureen O'Connor for their creative skills and hard work;

To the Office of Global Awareness and the Office of Global Education of the Worldwide Ministries Division and the Office of Stewardship and Mission Interpretation of the Congregational Ministries Division for their belief in the project and for their financial support.

Finally, none of this could have happened without the steadfast love of a nurturing God who could bring the seeds planted by our partner churches and watered by the International Leadership Development Program to bud, and then to glorious bloom!

—The Editor

PREFACE

My brother and I took a walk together recently. He is John McClure, a Presbyterian preaching professor. John reminded me that basic preaching courses often include instruction on how to lift up "heroes and heroines of the faith" in sermons. He reminisced about how missionaries inspired him when he was little. And he asked, "How can the church continue to benefit from stories and Christian role models from mission fields today?"

One of the answers we discussed is in this book. Here you will find some of the heroes and heroines today's mission personnel want you to know about. Here we introduce you to some of the colleagues whose development as leaders we helped to foster, and who have become our guides and mentors and supervisors in our mission work.

The title of this book comes from 1 Corinthians 3:6–9, which begins, "I planted, Apollos watered, but God gave the increase." The agricultural metaphor is the same one we use when we say "mission fields." The stories here reveal the huge number and variety of planters and waterers, both in the United States and in other countries. On the U.S.-based side, you will recognize references to mission personnel, seminaries, conference centers, congregations, middle governing bodies, and many General Assembly Council programs, as well as Presbyterian Women. In other countries, where U.S. Presbyterians are related to churches and institutions through partnerships coordinated through the Worldwide Ministries Division, the planters and waterers are at least as diverse.

A water bearer common to every one of these stories is our International Leadership Development program. Please read this book's "Introduction," "A Glimpse of the Future," and "Epilogue: A Note of Celebration and an Invitation" for information about this program and how to support it.

God has called and inspired all of us for the vast work of planting and watering represented by these stories. And God "gave the increase" through the lives of these faithful servants who answered particular calls to ministries in specific places and times. Thank you for your part in these stories, and for your prayers for "the increase."

Marian McClure, Director
Worldwide Ministries Division

INTRODUCTION

As plans were being made for the 1998 Year with Education, when Presbyterians would be asked to celebrate the transforming power of education in lives here and around the world, I was busy preparing with my husband to lift high the work of global education. Digging through old files and reviewing current programs, I gradually became aware that during the last fifty years an amazing story had been written—but not told!

In 1942 Dr. John Mackay, the president of Princeton Seminary, arose in a session of the Presbyterian Church in the U.S.A. Board of Foreign Missions to say that the time was at hand for the board to launch a long-range program for the training of young leaders of the related overseas national churches.[1] Since that time some three thousand leaders in partner churches around the world have been awarded scholarships for pursuing the educational goals dictated by the urgent tasks of ministry and mission in their national churches, indeed in their nations. I was reminded as I looked at the names how often, as Milan Opočenský has said, "Church history and national history . . . coincide, overlap and intersect."

I couldn't believe it! As I went through the list of names, I recognized moderators of national churches, seminary presidents, caring pastors, pioneer doctors in their fields, gifted and creative church musicians, and internationally known ecumenists and theologians. More unbelievable was the fact that the very people who had made this program possible, the people in the pews of American churches, giving faithfully to mission year after year, knew little or nothing of this story.

It was at that moment that this book was born. What more appropriate way to celebrate the Year with Education than to celebrate the results of this fifty-year partnership in international leadership development by telling its story! What follows are portraits of only a few of those remarkable leaders of the past half century. You will see the names and faces of others in your *Mission Yearbook for Prayer & Study,* in stories about great ecumenical conferences, and in the histories being written about the church around the world, and you will know that as American Presbyterians you have had a part in writing that history!

But the story hasn't ended! History is still being written. At this moment over one hundred young leaders are preparing to serve their churches in the coming century. Two-thirds of this number are studying here in the United States. A glimpse of their idealism and their vision for the church of the future is caught in the final pages of this book.

And you are still needed to continue this amazing program of leadership development to train tomorrow's leaders! As you read, consider ways to tell your congregation about this program and urge them to give to Extra Commitment Opportunity fund #132342. You will not only be celebrating the Year with Education; you will be preparing for the transforming work of the church of Jesus Christ in the twenty-first century!

June Ramage Rogers, Missionary-in-Residence, Year with Education, Office of Global Education and International Leadership Development

NOTE

1. Margaret Flory, "Walking in One Company," *Church & Society* (November/December 1986–January/February 1987).

Katalin Zsi'ros Bartha and Tibor Bartha, Jr.: A Remarkable Couple

by Robert C. Lodwick

I n 1987–1988 Tibor and Katalin Bartha of the Reformed Church in Hungary were invited by the Presbyterian Church (U.S.A.) to participate in the Leadership Development and Presbyterian Peacemaking Programs in the United States. It was a most propitious time for the Presbyterian Church to have the Barthas here. Many people still believed the conservative propaganda that there were no Christians behind the Iron Curtain and if there were, they were thought to have been collaborators with the Communist regime.

It was also the period of *glasnost* and *perestroika* in the Soviet Union—terms that needed definition by those who actually lived in the eastern half of Europe. The Barthas were much sought after as speakers in the Presbyterian Church, in ecumenical settings, and with civic groups where they were itinerated.

At the same time, the Barthas had an opportunity to learn about the Presbyterian Church, its role in peacemaking, and the role of women in the life of our churches. To some extent, they were even introduced to feminist theology, which had yet to become a part of theological discourse in Hungary.

Their team ministry, which required imagination and vision during the Communist era and during this period of freedom, is a fascinating story.

Fourteen months before the end of the Second World War, on March 16, 1944, Tibor Bartha was born in the Hungarian town of Munkacs, where his father was parish pastor. As a "child of the manse," Tibor had a childhood enriched by the glorious history of the Reformed faith, but also conditioned by the nation's struggles to recover from a devastating war and to learn to live under Communist rule. Hungary fought in support of Nazi Germany but by December of 1944 had surrendered to the Soviet army as it advanced along the Eastern Front and encircled Budapest. The Soviet military government ensured that all important positions in the defeated nation were occupied by loyal Communists, some of whom had escaped to Moscow in the 1930s.

By mid-1949, after the monarchy was abolished and a republic proclaimed, the Hungarian Communist Party had consolidated its power under the direction of the Soviet Union, power held until the summer of 1989. When Tibor was twelve, the student-led Revolution of 1956 was seen as a glimmer of hope against an oppressive government, but that resistance to Soviet hegemony was brutally extinguished.

It was after the aborted revolution that Tibor's father, the Rev. Tibor Bartha, Sr., became the presiding bishop of the Reformed Church in Hungary (RCH). In spite of strict government controls, the Communists were never able to snuff out the strong faith of a core community of committed Christians.

While two of the four theological seminaries were closed, the ones in Budapest and in Debrecen were permitted to remain open, although their scope was limited by the number of new students allowed to enroll each year. It was in the Reformed Theological Academy of Debrecen that Tibor Bartha enrolled in 1962 and was recognized as a student with great potential. Upon completion of these studies, he had the opportunity for additional study at Frederick Alexander University of Erlangen-Nürnberg, Germany, where he completed his doctorate, and later at Westminster College, Cambridge, England, for postdoctoral studies. The church has been grateful that Tibor had these opportunities. They helped prepare him for his future distinguished service in the church. Tibor married Katalin Zsi'ros, an ordained pastor of the Reformed Church in Hungary.

Tibor Bartha, Jr., served as deputy minister and then senior minister of the Reformed Church of Esztergom from 1974 to 1981, when he and Katalin were called to the Kálvin Square Church of Szeged, where they still serve as co-pastors. Esztergom is the See of the Archbishop of Esztergom, the Roman Catholic Primate of Hungary and head of the Hungarian Bishops' Synod. Being the Reformed pastor in Esztergom has historical significance for both the Catholic and Reformed churches. The Barthas have always had an ecumenical dimension to their ministry.

Pastors in Hungary never have just one job or one parish. Because of the shortage of pastors, they often have double or triple assignments. In addition to Esztergom and then Szeged, Tibor taught biblical Greek and New Testament studies at the Theological Seminary of the Hungarian Free Churches, where students from the minority Protestant churches such as the Baptist, Adventist, Methodist, and different Pentecostal groups are educated. This significant assignment lasted from 1973 to 1990 when, in the changing political situation, these churches were able to make other arrangements and Tibor had other responsibilities to add to his work.

The call to Szeged, a town situated on the Tisza River near the Hungarian border of Yugoslavia and Romania, meant a call to a crucial congregation in a "hot spot." They had and continue to have a very diverse ministry in this large city.

As events unfolded in the summer and fall of 1989, Hungary was the first country of the Eastern Bloc to open its frontiers toward the west. In November, the Berlin Wall fell and, shortly thereafter, the nations of eastern Europe and their churches were freed from the isolation experienced under the Communists. By 1990 the Hungarian Parliament had passed an action declaring freedom of conscience and religion as basic human rights, with the undisturbed practice of these rights guaranteed by the Hungarian Republic.

New spheres of activities were opened to the churches, Catholic and Protestant. They were free to build new parishes, particularly in the burgeoning cities. Once again the churches could play a key role in education and many of their former schools were returned to their jurisdiction. The church could provide chaplains for the army and for prisons, something never permitted under Communist rule. They could expand their social ministries. While tensions between church and state did not dissolve overnight, representatives of each continued an open dialogue.

The Barthas were well prepared to launch new programs to meet the challenges of this period in the life of the church. Tibor became an active prison chaplain. Szeged has a high security prison and Tibor has undertaken to address the spiritual needs of these prisoners. Because of his effectiveness, he serves as senior minister of the RCH Committee for Pastoral Care in Prisons.

In 1992, Tibor was appointed professor of the Faculty of Religious Education and Teacher Training in Szeged. This program is training teachers to be religious education teachers in the school system, public and private. In 1993 he was the general editor of the *Christian Biblical Lexicon*. His colleagues agree that it is "a wonderful compendium and explanation of biblical expressions and Bible-related words. Without his managing and editing skills, this extraordinary work would not have become a reality."

Recently he has prepared a bilateral agreement between the church and the principals of different colleges and universities in Szeged to introduce a ministry to students and faculty. This is the second such campus ministry in Hungary.

Tibor's activities have meant that Katalin has been responsible for a great portion of the parish work of the Kávin Square congregation, which she has carried out in an effective and efficient way. She is a fine preacher and pastoral counselor.

The Presbyterian Church (U.S.A.) has been enriched by the presence of the Barthas in its midst and continues to follow their rich ministries with prayers and encouragement.

Robert C. Lodwick is former Secretary of Education, United Presbyterian Church in the U.S.A., and former Area Coordinator for Europe, Worldwide Ministries Division, Presbyterian Church (U.S.A.).

Norman Bent:
A Mediator in the Midst of Both Sides

by Margaret D. Wilde

In 1964, when Norman Bent began his ministry in the Moravian Church on the Atlantic Coast of Nicaragua, his was a lonely voice against racism and social injustice in that region. His people—the Miskito, Sumu, Rama, and Garifuna Indians, and the English-speaking, Afro-Caribbean Creoles—were ruled by the Somoza dictatorship in far-off Managua with callous disregard for their needs and abilities. Most of the schools and medical care available to them were provided by the Moravian Church; with 80 percent of the coastal people as members, the church was also the only social institution rooted in their communities. But the church was not yet paying much attention to their economic needs, their growing sense of ethnic identity, or the political and social injustice of their situation.

In 1974 the church became an autonomous province of the worldwide Moravian Unity, and spurred by Norman's vision, it began to address these issues. He became the first director of the Social Action Committee of the Moravian Church (CASIM), working with local communities on agricultural, forestry, fishing, nutrition, and popular education projects. He was the right person for that job: in a region of diverse and often isolated cultures, he was of both Creole and Miskito ancestry and had grown up in the multicultural village of Tasbapounie. He had also studied theology in Costa Rica, where he came to appreciate the dominant Spanish-speaking culture, the ecumenical movement, and the prophetic role to which the church was called in the face of poverty and racism throughout Latin America.

While CASIM was beginning its work in community development, an Indian rights movement was emerging in the Miskito and Sumu communities. The church was supportive of the movement, and local pastors were among its key leaders. Local authorities occasionally harassed both CASIM and the Indian organization, but the central government was more concerned with the

Sandinista uprising in western Nicaragua that would overthrow Somoza in 1979.

From the outset the Sandinistas recognized the strategic importance of the Atlantic Coast; they feared that Somoza supporters and their U.S. allies would use the church and the Indian movement to undermine the new government. The fear of Indian militancy soon became self-fulfilling; harsh government actions prompted many Miskito leaders to take up arms, with widespread support in their communities and covert aid from the United States. The church, however, sought to promote understanding on both sides. With the support of the two Moravian bishops and other pastors, Norman helped to negotiate a transition of local authority and a peaceful settlement in several incidents between the new officials and the communities.

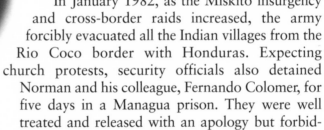

Norman Bent

In January 1982, as the Miskito insurgency and cross-border raids increased, the army forcibly evacuated all the Indian villages from the Rio Coco border with Honduras. Expecting church protests, security officials also detained Norman and his colleague, Fernando Colomer, for five days in a Managua prison. They were well treated and released with an apology but forbidden to return to the Atlantic Coast for a year. Norman was transferred from CASIM to the pastorate of the Moravian congregation in Managua. There he became the church's main contact with concerned visitors from around the world and a widely respected interpreter of the situation to church groups in Europe and North America.

Norman focused very intentionally on the art of peacemaking during this time. He said at a Mennonite consultation in 1986: "As a mediator I discovered that my role was in the middle of both sides and I had to look at both sides as enemy because both sides mistrusted my role. . . . Being an indigenous person I felt closer to that side, the group of Nicaraguans who have suffered most. On the other hand, I also saw the other side as Nicaraguan brothers and sisters who were struggling for a dream, a dream that we all want to be a part of, a dream for a more just society."

Negotiations between the Sandinista government and the Miskito insurgency began that year, with mediation and logistical support from Norman and other church leaders. The process was slow and frustrating; the Atlantic Coast was no longer the Sandinistas' priority concern. Eventually a system of regional autonomy was established and the insurgents invited to participate in the 1990 elections. The negotiations ended without formal settlement when the Sandinistas were defeated in those elections. The new government persuaded the insurgents to lay down their arms by promising financial aid for resettlement and postwar reconstruction.

Then came Norman's opportunity to fulfill his long-deferred hope for more advanced study. With scholarship assistance from the Presbyterian Church (U.S.A.) and a pastoral appointment by the United Church of Canada, in 1992 he and his family moved to Winnipeg, Canada, where he received a master of sacred theology degree in 1994. As a secular university with a school of theology, Winnipeg University offered two courses of special interest: one that emphasized the spiritual traditions of Native Americans and one on conflict resolution.

He also enjoyed serving on the pastoral team at Regent Park United Church, which welcomed his family and gave them many opportunities to share their experiences. But there was still work to do at home, he said: "God has used my wife (Modestina) to influence my life so that together we could accept the call from the church in Nicaragua and return home."

Nicaragua was not a happy place in 1994. The promises made in 1990 had been forgotten; the central government neither understood nor cared about the Atlantic Coast; many former insurgents had turned to banditry; and the continuing economic decline left little hope for postwar reconstruction. But Norman returned to his congregation with renewed pastoral energy. The needs of his people were deeper than ever, and he had a special gift for encouraging and supporting the young pastors who came to Managua to study.

In 1995 Norman was called by the Latin American Council of Churches (CLAI) to head its pastoral program for work with black and Indian communities. Based in Managua, where he continues to serve the local congregation, he now also leads consultations throughout Latin America on the problems of racism and the resources of native spirituality. After two years in this dual role, he says, "I find much joy in what I am doing."

New challenges await the people and church on the Atlantic Coast. Miskito insurgents began taking up arms again in March 1998, demanding action on the promises of resettlement and reconstruction assistance, and

The Atlantic Coast of Nicaragua

ewing the claims of land and autonomy that they fought for in the 1980s. There is hope for a more peaceful outcome this time: the people have a stronger sense of their ethnic identity, rights, and spiritual resources, and the church is more confidently taking the initiative in mediation. Strengthened by his studies and continuing dialogue with concerned Christians in North and South America, Norman will continue to help the church follow that dream.

Margaret D. Wilde, writer, teacher, and consultant on peacemaking and human rights, has worked with the Nicaraguan Moravian Church periodically since 1977. She currently lives in Miami, Florida.

"I must attribute to the program we have known as Leadership Development the place of our church's most significant educational contribution in which I have been involved."

Alan Hamilton, one of the initiators of the Leadership Development Program and former professor and counselor at the Latin American Biblical Seminary in Costa Rica

Feliciano V. Cariño: Uniquely Prepared for Ecumenical Leadership

by Louise Palm and Cobbie Palm

O n a rainy August day in 1962, a group of twenty-five international students, participants in an ecumenical study seminar, were gathered in the Protestant Chapel on the campus of the University of the Philippines in Quezon City. They listened intently as a young Filipino leader in the Philippine Student Christian Movement spoke passionately about oppression and hope in his country and throughout Asia. His name was Feliciano Cariño. His prophetic words and interpretations of Filipino politics and culture caused everyone to listen with respect. The group traveled throughout the Philippines, meeting with political and religious leaders, among them Congressman Benigno Aquino, who would later play a pivotal role in the Philippine political drama.

Feliciano Cariño, Fely, as he is known to his friends, was at the threshold of an important career as an ecumenical church leader. The following year, through the Commission on World Mission of the National Student Christian Federation, Fely was invited to spend one year as an intern in the United States, working with Margaret Flory and the Presbyterian Office of Student World Relations. Students across this country came to know him, and once again, his prophetic words brought the voice of the Philippine student movement to an international audience.

Always a charismatic and competent leader, Fely was invited to become part of the staff of the Office of Student World Relations of the Presbyterian Church (U.S.A.). This was a period during which the Commission on Ecumenical Mission and Relations (COEMAR) intensified its policies of mutuality in mission and the internationalization of staff positions. Fely, as one of the bright stars on the horizon, soon became the executive secretary of the Office of Student World Relations, a position he held until 1972. Throughout these years he played a critical leadership role in the national Student Christian Movement, which was going through the difficult times that all student movements experienced during the turbulent 1960s.

By 1972 the Presbyterian Church was in the midst of a traumatic restructuring. Thus, it was a natural progression for Fely, now well-known in international student circles, to be called to Geneva, Switzerland, as the general secretary of the World Student Christian Federation. From his office in Geneva, he traveled throughout the world for the next four years.

During his time in the United States Fely, who was an excellent student, completed his PhD at Princeton Theological Seminary with the assistance of the Presbyterian Leadership Development Program.

But one cannot always be a "student" and always be on a journey far from home, so in 1977, fifteen years after he left, Fely was ready to return and continue his ministry in the Philippines. He and his wife, Theresa,

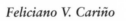

Feliciano V. Cariño

became involved at once in the anti-Marcos movement of which the United Church of Christ in the Philippines was a very strong advocate. He spent these early years back in the Philippines as a faculty member and later served as dean of the Philippine Christian University.

In 1987 Dr. Feliciano Cariño was elected to serve as general secretary of the National Council of Churches in the Philippines (NCCP), a position he held until 1996. As a leader of the Protestant community in the Philippines, he took an active part in the rise of the People's Movement of the mid-80s, leading to the end of the Marcos dictatorship. He continued to speak passionately and act forcefully on behalf of the peace process during the fragile Corazon Aquino presidency and even into the Ramos administration. He was recognized as one who spoke on sound theological grounds, and he became an important theologian for his own church, the United Church of Christ of the Philippines.

It was while fulfilling the task as a member of the peace process commissioned by the Ramos administration that his abilities were recognized by the Philippine government. Subsequently, this led to his invitation to be a member of the government panel in the continuing effort to bring resolution to the ongoing conflict between the National Democratic Front and the Philippine government. When he assumed his role on the government panel, his role as the spokesperson for the NCCP Peace Program gradually diminished and eventually stopped, even while he continued as the general secretary of the National Council of Churches in the Philippines.

Dr. Cariño's ecumenical experience and leadership, along with his knowledge of the world church that began with the international Study Seminar in 1962, made him uniquely prepared for his present leadership role in the Christian Conference of Asia. He describes the challenge of his five-year appointment as general secretary of the Christian Conference of Asia (CCA):

> CCA in itself is a vision. As vision, it is not yet reality. As vision it includes the hope of a comprehensive and inclusive fellowship of churches in Asia, acting together in obedience to God's mission in the context of the changing and ever-challenging economic, social, political, and religious life of Asia, and hoping to make an Asian contribution to the wider, worldwide ecumenical movement.

That vision is becoming reality as the CCA sharpens the Asian theological agenda toward the twenty-first century through the formation of the Congress of Asian Theologians (CATS) and makes more comprehensive the fellowship of Asian churches by strengthening relationships with the Roman Catholic Church in the region and encouraging participation of evangelical churches. CCA would thus become an Asian Conference of Church and Society that would review ecumenical social ethics, and project work in the widening and changing arenas of social witness in Asia; sponsor an Asian round table on mission and missiology that would review ecumenical missiology, analyze current problems, and project "a third generation of missiology" drawn from the experience of Asian churches and organizations; and plan a major Asian gathering of youth and students that would provide the basis for new leadership for the future.

Student leader, theologian, churchman, and ecumenical visionary, Feliciano V. Cariño is a model of Christian leadership in our time.

Louise Palm is a former mission worker in the Philippines. This was written with the help of her son, Cobbie Palm, currently a mission worker in the Philippines.

João Dias de Araújo:
A Voice for Ecumenism and Reform

by Peter Kemmerle and William W. Rogers

João Dias de Araújo is one of the heroes of the Presbyterian Church. In the 1960s, when Brazil was caught in the throes of the cold war and the historic Presbyterian Church in that country was tearing itself apart, Dias was among those who kept their heads and stood up for the values of an open society and a compassionate church. Not only was Dias a man with the courage of his convictions, he was also an extraordinary leader who inspired confidence in those among whom he stood. Perhaps most notable among his achievements was his role in the founding of a new church, the United Presbyterian Church of Brazil, and his service, twice, as its moderator. But that's getting ahead of our story.

Dias was born into a family of Presbyterians. His grandfather was an elder. He hosted the first Presbyterian missionaries to arrive in the frontier territory of Mato Grosso in 1920. His father was a pastor for forty years. One of seven brothers and sisters, Dias grew up in Mato Grosso. At the age of sixteen his father became pastor of the Presbyterian Church of Caetité in the State of Bahia in Northeast Brazil.

"To understand my ministry," say Dias, "you have to know something about the Northeast. It is the poorest part of Brazil, and though it was the first part of Brazil to be settled by the Portuguese colonists, it is the least developed economically. In the middle of the Northeast is a huge, semiarid region we call the *sertão*, which means 'backlands.' Life is always hard in the *sertão*, but when there is a drought—and we usually have a three-year drought every fifteen years or so—it is almost impossible. The land almost literally burns up, and those who live in the backlands must flee. Many simply die of thirst and hunger. Shortly after my family moved to the Northeast, I went south to go to school. During vacations I would make the long trip back home to see my family. Each trip took several days, first by train and then in the back of a truck. During these trips my traveling companions were migrants from the *sertão* who were on the road for a different reason: their survival depended on it. In the south of Brazil these migrants were looked down upon, and this increased my desire to do something." Dias laughs with fondness when he remembers the title of his youthful book of poetry, *They Are Also Brazilians.* "Of course, at the time, I thought it was the drought that caused the emigration," says Dias. "Later I came to see that it was the agrarian structure itself."

After finishing seminary in 1953, Dias and his wife, Ithamar, moved to Ponte Nova, a small town in the *sertão* founded by Presbyterian mission workers. Five of their six children were born there while Dias was pastor of the Presbyterian church.

In 1960 Dias moved his family to the port city of Recife, the largest in Northeast Brazil, where he had been invited to join the faculty of the Presbyterian Seminary. He taught systematic theology and Christian ethics. While in Recife he became involved in the two movements that would define his ministry over the next four decades: ecumenism and agrarian reform. He was active in a number of ecumenical organizations in Recife, in which the progressive Catholic archbishop, Dom Helder Camara, was also active. At the same time he was a collaborator with the Peasant Leagues, early and important proponents of agrarian reform.

João Dias de Araújo

The military coup in 1964 changed Dias's life, as it changed the lives of most Brazilians. Cold war anticommunist rhetoric came to be the only acceptable discourse within the Presbyterian Church of Brazil (IPB). Dias's support of ecumenism and reform and his unwillingness to be silent made him *persona non grata* in the increasingly conservative church.

"My scholarship to study at Princeton in 1966 came just at the right time," says Dias. "I was under pressure from the military government, and Princeton was a good place to clarify my ideas and do some research while things cooled down in Brazil. Princeton proved to be very important to me. You could say that Princeton gave Calvin back to me. Presbyterian missionaries in Brazil had received their understanding of Calvin directly or indirectly from the conservative, nineteenth-century theologian Charles Hodge. These missionaries were our teachers and they taught Calvin without any emphasis on his social ethics—noncritical Calvin, in other words." Dias's year at Princeton gave him more than Calvin. It introduced him to Karl Barth and Reinhold Niebuhr—theologians who were giving Christians all over the world the tools for the intellectual challenges of the midcentury, yet who were virtually unknown in missionary Brazil.

In 1970 Dias was expelled from the Presbyterian seminary in Recife without explanation. "They just told me that 'It's not in the interest of the church to have future pastors receive orientation from pastors like you.' Church leaders at the time were very friendly with the military dictatorship and permitted no dissent. Hundreds of pastors were expelled and the whole movement for a more open church and a more just society was closed down."

Later Dias wrote *Inquisitions Without Burnings*, which described the transformation of the Presbyterian Church of Brazil from mainstream to fundamentalist orthodoxy. With his career as a seminary professor apparently finished, he went to law school and prepared to help the rural workers of the Northeast in their struggle for land. In 1975 he returned to rural Bahia and worked with peasant groups to defend their rights. He later founded CEDITER, the Evangelical Commission for Land Rights.

Eight years after his expulsion from the seminary, Dias and other Presbyterians founded the United Presbyterian Church of Brazil (IPU), from its beginning committed to ecumenism, human rights, and the ministry of women as pastors and elders. In 1986 Dias realized a lifelong dream when he and others founded an ecumenical seminary, the Institute for Theological Education in Bahia (ITEBA). It has turned out to be a remarkable achievement.

Dias is clearly a man who, with the help of God and through his own courage, brilliance, and Christian commitment, made himself. But clearly, too, his remarkable career has come "with a little help from his friends." Among his many friends he counts the Presbyterian Church (U.S.A.) and those responsible for its Leadership Development Program.

Peter Kemmerle, a former mission worker in Brazil, is now with the Mission Connections Program, Worldwide Ministries Division, PC(USA).

William W. Rogers, a former mission worker in Brazil, now a retired pastor, is currently a Missionary-in-Residence, Year with Education, Office of Global Education and International Leadership Development, Worldwide Ministries Division, PC(USA).

Maitland Evans:
A Man of Vision and Faith

by Lewin L. Williams

In the few moments when Maitland Evans is allowed to be quiet and reflective (and that is mostly on a plane going somewhere), he dreams yet another dream, and before long he has worked out a structure by which it may become a reality. Maitland Evans was born in Jackson Town, a district in rural Trelawny, Jamaica. While still a teenager, Maitland was referred to by his pastor, a missionary from Britain, as his "little Timothy." Having already made a significant impression on the pastor, he conducted Bible classes throughout the First Hill Charge (parish). Knowing the family Maitland grew up in, I am not astonished that he became so conversant with the Bible at such an early age.

There were six children born to his parents, three girls and three boys. Maitland was the fourth child. There was Bible study every night at home, where Maitland developed the skills of Bible interpretation. By the time I met him he already had aspirations for the ministry. I was a first-year student in the seminary and always received a barrage of questions from Maitland about the ministry. Rumor has it that something I said made him delay entering seminary until after my graduation. We speak of it jokingly even now, that he was afraid that I would personally teach him the way of *tapeinos* through the *paradosis* (seminary talk!)

After graduating from the seminary with an LTh and a BA in theology, Maitland served a very rural charge that gave him time for serious reflection. During his second charge, which was not quite as rural as the first, he was demonstrating such clarity in articulation that people were forced to sit up and listen. That light was being shed on his ministry and his role in society has been an inspiration not only in the United Church in Jamaica and the Cayman Islands but also on the international scene, wherever there are deliberations on partnership and the "equipping of saints."

Maitland has placed four indelible marks in time on the history of the church: the shaping of the London-based Council for World Missions (CWM), Training in Mission (TIM), the Institute for Theological and Leadership Development (ITLD), and the Mel Nathan Institute.

COUNCIL FOR WORLD MISSION

Noted for reciprocity in mission, CWM has transformed the traditional North to South model of mission. The new South-to-South, South-to-North, and subsequent, alternative North-to-South missionary ventures owe their success to the genius of Maitland Evans. In the 1970s

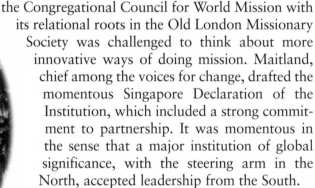

the Congregational Council for World Mission with its relational roots in the Old London Missionary Society was challenged to think about more innovative ways of doing mission. Maitland, chief among the voices for change, drafted the momentous Singapore Declaration of the Institution, which included a strong commitment to partnership. It was momentous in the sense that a major institution of global significance, with the steering arm in the North, accepted leadership from the South.

The Council for World Mission did not change easily, however. New ideas with old personnel do not always add up to successful change, especially if the new ideas do not originate with

Maitland Evans

the old personnel. Yet it is to the credit of the Council for World Mission that it issued a call to Maitland to move to its head office in London with a mandate to put the new theories into practice. From 1981 through 1982 he served the organization as its secretary for Education in Mission. Later he became the chairperson and served for two terms, during which time his views on partnership among churches took on international significance. Until 1993 Maitland Evans played the pivotal role in the shaping of CWM on the world stage.

TRAINING IN MISSION

Although it was Gwen Cashmore who made the passionate plea at the CWM Council meeting in Hong Kong in 1979 for a commitment to a new venture in the preparation for and the practice of mission, it was Maitland's idea, and the program continues to this day.

It has gathered young representatives of partner churches from Africa, New Zealand, Kiribati, Myanmar, Papua New Guinea, Korea, Jamaica, India, United Kingdom, Guyana, the Netherlands, Madagascar, Taiwan, Samoa, South Africa, and Australia, along with guests from places such as the United States, Canada, and El Salvador. These young people are thrown together and placed at risk by the bane or blessing of culture shock. They have usually spent four months in England, followed by six months in Jamaica training in theology, experiencing at the same time the social mix of northern and southern cultures. They never return to their own countries the same.

This program became the practical demonstration of how partnership works among the people of God.

THE INSTITUTE FOR THEOLOGICAL AND LEADERSHIP DEVELOPMENT

Maitland Evans is a committed connectionalist with a firm belief that the congregation is an important missionary agent, that no policy is truly transmitted through the church *except* through the agency of the congregation. As such, he is also a congregationalist at heart. Yet he doesn't see the congregation as a separate entity from the denomination, which holds the responsibility for the shaping of the congregation as the agent of mission. Hence, from 1985 onward, Maitland designed and implemented the strategy for the restructuring of the United Church, his own denomination, with the importance of the congregation in mind.

The center piece of ministry and mission is the Institute for Theological and Leadership Development. When most church persons in the Caribbean use the term "local," they mean territory. When Maitland uses it he means "congregation." For him, the congregation is the hub around which the denomination turns. The ITLD, therefore, created a teaching base out of the congregation where student and congregation together become conscious agents of mission. Instead of moving the student into a seminary setting, the teacher comes to the student and makes a seminary out of the congregation. Such revolutionary approaches to theological and leadership education are the product of a fertile and keen mind, totally dedicated to the mission of the church. Maitland is such a person.

THE MEL NATHAN INSTITUTE

The institute is named after Maitland's father, Melvin Nathan Evans, who died while Maitland was a teenager. In fact, it represents more than a naming opportunity. Launched officially in 1978 in one of the most depressed and hopeless areas of Kingston-Hannah Town, the institute is a pledge to model its operations after a father who seemed to acquire in order to give to the needy.

Mel Nathan is the practical product of Maitland's master's thesis at Harvard. In it he envisioned a program that did more than supply handouts to the poor. His dream was of a program organized for self-sufficiency, in order that persons could become self-actualized. The program looked very good on paper, and one of Maitland's professors challenged him to make it a reality. And, by God, he did.

Mel Nathan is now a training facility that has provided academic and nutritional "head starts" for deprived children, retraining for convicts reentering society, skills in motor mechanics, culinary art, arts and crafts, fabric tailoring, and even farming.

In the country of Jamaica, where personhood may be measured by one's possessions, it is refreshing to know someone whose noteworthiness is dependent on his dedication to church and community. In the benevolent achievements that resulted from a dedication as husband, father, church worker, community leader, and educator, Maitland has given himself without reserve and has asked for nothing in return.

Lewin L. Williams is a mission worker, as is his wife Joyce. He is a professor at the United Theological College of the West Indies, where he lectures on contemporary trends in theology.

Editor's Note: Dr. Maitland Evans was a recent keynoter at the St. Louis Conference on Congregations in Global Mission, thus demonstrating partnership in mission from the South to the North and the importance of the local congregation in global mission. A graduate of the United Theological College of the West Indies and Harvard University's School of Education, Maitland was most recently supported in his studies by the Presbyterian Church (U.S.A.) for continuing education in counseling and community development at the University of Birmingham in the United Kingdom.

João Wilson Faustini:
The Watershed in Brazilian Protestant Music

by Eber F. Silveira Lima

I t can be said that João Wilson Faustini gave body to sacred Brazilian Protestant music, retrieving it from mere repetition and simple translations of music originating outside the country. Indeed he gave choral music a Brazilian identity. And all of that with great technical ability and artistry! Though Protestant music in Brazil currently finds itself caught between traditional hymns and the new songs of charismatic communities—or struggling to find a place for the instruments used in popular music along with the traditional instruments found in Protestant worship—it recognizes in João Wilson Faustini one of its major influences.

Born on November 20, 1931, in the city of Bariri, in the interior of the state of São Paulo, Faustini, the grandson of Italian immigrants, knew poverty as a child. From the nineteenth century onward, Italian immigration to Brazil was extensive. Many immigrants came to serve as farm laborers, replacing slave labor. João's Italian grandparents were among those who arrived in Brazil soon after the abolition of slavery in 1888. His paternal grandfather was converted after reading the parable of the rich man and Lazarus.

When Faustini was eight years old and heard the choir of the Protestant Musical Caravan, a group of students and preachers of the José Manoel da Conceição Institute from Jandira, he was fascinated. Created by several denominations, including the PC(USA), represented by the Rev. William Alfred Waddell, the institute prepared young people to follow careers as ministers of the Word. The caravans were a way of recruiting young people for church vocations. At eleven, the young João was already singing in the choir of the Independent Presbyterian Church in Pirajui in the interior of the state of São Paulo; at twelve, he felt called to the ministry; at sixteen he directed the choir of the church in Osasco, near São Paulo.

At eighteen, João entered the institute, where he had the opportunity to learn from a great American Presbyterian musician, Evelina Harper. Subsequently, he was moved to continue his studies at Westminster Choir

College, where he received a bachelor's degree in music in 1955. While studying in the United States, he sang in the Westminster Symphonic Choir, under
the direction of maestros like Leopold Stokowski. In that same year, he
assumed the post that was formerly held by Evalina Harper
and led the Protestant Musical Caravan throughout the
country. By the grace of God he was now directing
the group and the choir that had inspired him so
many years before as a child.

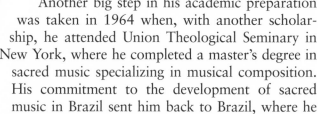

During the next ten years, Faustini was active
in the preparation of directors, organists, and
musicians for Brazilian Protestant churches. He
organized choral festivals and workshops about
sacred music, popularizing sacred music for
local church choirs, not only for Presbyterians.

Another big step in his academic preparation
was taken in 1964 when, with another scholarship, he attended Union Theological Seminary in
New York, where he completed a master's degree in
sacred music specializing in musical composition.

João Wilson Faustini   His commitment to the development of sacred
music in Brazil sent him back to Brazil, where he
organized the Department of Music at the Theological Seminary of the
Independent Church of Brazil in São Paulo. His work was so admired that in
April 1975, the Presbytery of São Paulo ordained him as minister of music, the
first in Brazil. In the years following, he worked as minister of music in São
Paulo and in Rio de Janeiro. He also taught at the Southern Baptist Seminary in
Rio, the largest of that denomination in South America.

The work of João Wilson Faustini can be classified as extraordinary if we
consider all of his publications, compositions, translations, and musical
arrangements. Since 1955, he has produced work of the highest quality, trans-
lating and adapting choral music for general church use. In order to provide
music of this quality, Faustini and others founded Evelina Harper Protestant
Religious Publications, which today operates under the auspices of the
Protestant Society of Sacred Music (SOEMUS). SOEMUS was founded in
1990 to promulgate in Brazil a ministry of sacred music and to reunite students of Faustini and others who had been inspired by his work. *The Heavens
Proclaim* was the first publication that related music to liturgy and included
worship resources (choral responses, and so forth), organizing the contents

according to the liturgical calendar.

As Protestant music in Brazil became more informal, Faustini was the pioneer in publishing a quality work for young people, *Hinos Contemporaneos 1971* (Contemporary Hymns), which was repeated some years later as *Sempre Louvarei* (1982). Another innovative work, a trilingual hymnal (Portuguese, Spanish, and English), *Seja Louvado*, was organized with his brothers Zwinglio and Loyde in 1972. It included Brazilian hymns alongside favorite traditional hymns. This work included liturgical helps at the end. Faustini himself authored several hymns well known in all the churches. He encouraged choral music in Brazil to the extent that he became the obligatory reference for all those who had anything to do with Protestant music.

Today, in spite of the increasing influence of charismatic music, which has significantly influenced the historic churches, Faustini continues to be respected. He conducts a workshop every year on sacred music in São Paulo. Recognizing the growth of choral music over forty years, Faustini noted: "When I began my ministry, there was no written music for choirs; in fact, there were very few choirs!" Faustini's participation modified that picture definitively. Protestant church music abounds in all of Brazil. About the current musical scene in the Brazilian Protestant church, Faustini laments: "Music has lost much of its reverence, dignity, and its theology. Entertainment and romantic pleasure appear to be the major objectives."

It is possible to divide Brazilian choral music into "before and after Faustini." The benefits of his long and productive career are clear. His work will remain for many future generations because he brought quality to sacred music, made it more accessible and certainly more contextual, and insisted that music sung in the church have liturgical significance. It is certainly not difficult to understand why Faustini is the most important name in Protestant Brazilian sacred music!

Rev. Eber F. Silveira Lima, a former student of Faustini, is a professor at the Theological Seminary of the Independent Presbyterian Church in Londrina, Brazil. He was Mission Partner-in-Residence to the Worldwide Ministries Division of the PC(USA) in Louisville from 1997 to 1998.

Written in Portuguese and translated from Portuguese to English by June Ramage Rogers

Samuel Habib:
A Force for Empowering Natural Leaders

by Harry Eberts

Samuel Habib of Egypt went into the small village of Herz in Upper Egypt more than forty-five years ago. What he found there and what he did with his discovery changed for the better the lives of millions of Egyptians in the half century to follow. The Egyptian mission of the United Presbyterian Church of North America sent Sam to that village to implement the "Each One Teach One" literacy program originated by Dr. Frank Laubach in India. Almost as soon as Sam entered Herz, he recognized that the problems of living that people faced were so great that teaching literacy alone would have little impact on their lives. Sam decided instead to institute a package of services to accomplish the task: teaching up-to-date farming techniques to the men and nutrition to the mothers, providing health care and clean water to everyone, and designing literacy programs for the entire village.

Along with this package of services, Sam made four fundamental decisions that affected his subsequent ministry. He would extend those privileges not to certain individuals in the village, but to every man, woman, and child who lived there. On an equal basis, with no distinctions made, he would serve both the Muslims and the Christians in the community. For these services he would charge whatever the person could pay—only a tiny *piaster* if that was all the person could afford. He did this so no individuals could ever consider themselves to be receiving charity, but would be contributing to their own well-being. He also determined that the teams of workers sent into the villages to deliver the services would be made up of both men and women in equal numbers.

But this vision had a price tag attached to it, and this price was too high for the Egyptian church alone to bear. So Sam appealed to the Presbyterians he had met while he was studying at the University of Syracuse and itinerating through churches in the United States. The national Presbyterian Women's Organization responded to his call with a grant of $30,000 to implement his vision, a gift that gave life to the Coptic Evangelical Organization for Social Services (CEOSS).

For fifteen years CEOSS delivered its services in an increasing number of poverty-stricken communities, and CEOSS as an organization grew. But Sam was observing a fact about the work that bothered him. CEOSS itself was making most of the decisions for its communities. "Not right," Sam said. Village people themselves need to make the decisions that affect their lives. So CEOSS changed its way of working. From that moment on, the first thing CEOSS workers did when they entered a new community—and they enter two or three new communities every year—was to search for the community's natural leaders (women and men, young and old) and empower them to make the vital decisions that determined the quality of life in the community. CEOSS's role changed. No longer was it a matter of delivering a preset package of programs. Its task now is to work with the people who make the decisions about community life and then to help find the resources to implement the programs that the village council selected.

Samuel Habib

This meant education and training and more education and training. Sam himself was educated in the schools of Egypt set up by the United Presbyterian Church and graduated from that church's seminary in Cairo. A leadership training grant from the church supported his studies at Syracuse and later helped him to earn a doctorate from San Francisco Theological Seminary. Sam insisted that training and education were the heart of his program. So he saw to it that people received proper training. These people included his own staff, the village workers, the people on the leadership council of the communities, the residents of the communities, ministers, elders, and members of the Coptic Evangelical Church (the Presbyterian Church in Egypt). Some were taught on site. Others were brought to the training center constructed at Itsa, 250 kilometers south of Cairo. Still others were directed to pursue their education in England, Canada, India, Korea, and the United States. Teach-teach-teach, plan-plan-plan, work-work-work, in every possible way to raise the quality of life of each person touched by CEOSS. As this ministry grew, the lives of 2 million Egyptians each year were directly improved by the organization that Samuel Habib instituted and directed.

In his last years, Sam began intentionally to reach out to the decision makers in the Egyptian Islamic community—Protestant ministers, Orthodox and Catholic priests, and Muslim *imams*—to discuss development in Egypt. Sam himself became the co-worker and friend of the Grand Mufti of Egypt. Westminster College in New Wilmington, Pennsylvania, a Presbyterian college with historic ties to Presbyterians in Egypt, offered honorary doctorates of peacemaking to Sam and the Grand Mufti on the same platform in January 1995. Government officials sought out CEOSS to learn from them what they had learned about improving the quality of the lives of the Egyptian people.

CEOSS leaders helped set the agenda for the worldwide "Population and Development" conference held in Cairo in the fall of 1995. In addition, they sent the women from the CEOSS staff to assist in the planning of the World Congress of Women held in China in 1996. When Sam died suddenly in 1997, he was busy setting up a dialogue center in Cairo where Christians and Muslims could meet, talk, think, and maybe someday pray together, to assist each of their historic communities of faith to understand more fully the other and, at the same time, to probe more deeply into the riches of its own faith.

Samuel Habib was born into and nurtured by the Presbyterian Church of Egypt. By the time he laid down his work, this church, and Christians and churches throughout the world, had been transformed by the vibrant ministry he helped to bring into being along the banks of the ever-flowing Nile.

Harry Eberts is a former professor at San Francisco Theological Seminary, a retired pastor, and longtime friend of Sam Habib.

"The Leadership Development ministry . . . remains as the most profound, long-term, unambiguously beneficial investment the United Presbyterian Church ever made."

Frederick R. Wilson, former Associate General Director for Ecumenical and Interchurch Relations, United Presbyterian Church in the U.S.A.

Riad and Rose Jarjour: A Unique Couple in a Shared Ecumenical Ministry

by Haydn White

R iad Jarjour is general secretary of the Middle East Council of Churches. His wife Rose is general secretary of the Fellowship of Middle East Evangelical Churches. If "unique" had a superlative form, the Jarjours would be one of the "most unique," if not "the most unique" couple working in the ecumenical Christian community. Riad and Rose became a couple by exchanging marriage vows in 1975 and have continued to dedicate their lives to the proclamation of the gospel, primarily through administrative and ecumenical ministries. It is hard to think of one member of this team without the other because, although they now have different portfolios, their ministry has truly been a cooperative enterprise.

Riad and Rose have been assisted by the Leadership Development Program of the Presbyterian Church (U.S.A.). They each began study at McCormick Theological Seminary while Dr. Esther Stine was associate for Leadership Development. Dr. Stine was an outstanding advocate of involving women from the third world in leadership positions and it is to her credit that Rose was given the opportunity to accompany Riad.

Riad was born in Aleppo, Syria, in 1948. He grew up in the industrial city of Homs, where his father worked in the Syrian Oil Company. While in high school, he spent one year in Green Bay, Wisconsin, as an exchange student. After completing his BA at Hagazian College in Beirut, Lebanon, and his MDiv at the Near East School of Theology, he served as a chaplain in South Lebanon in the Marjo'oun-Nabatiyyeh area for several years. There he operated a public reading room and developed strong relations with the local Muslim community. In 1978 he was ordained as a minister in the Evangelical Synod of Syria and Lebanon.

Rose was born in Brazil in 1954, but at the age of four her family moved to Syria. She completed her preparatory education and teacher training program in Syria and from 1971 to 1975 taught in elementary schools in Syria. After her marriage to Riad, she taught in the Evangelical School in South Lebanon and participated in ministry with Riad in the Shi'ite community in Nabatia, Lebanon. In 1982 she received a BA in Christian education from the Near East School of Theology.

From the time Riad was appointed the director of the Youth Program of the Middle East Council of Churches in 1978, it was obvious that the appointment was not for him alone but for Rose as well. This was recognized when they were both appointed as codirectors of the Ayia Napa Conference Center in Ayia Napa, Cyprus, in 1983. One only had to visit them to see that it was a team ministry with each having an equal share in responsibility. During the 1970s and 1980s the Ayia Napa Conference Center became a very significant place where Christians of various denominations and traditions could gather away from the turmoil of a war-torn Middle East.

Rose Jarjour

In 1983 and again in 1985 both Riad and Rose came to McCormick Theological Seminary in Chicago under the auspices of the Leadership Development Program of the Presbyterian Church. Riad came to study for a DMin degree and Rose for a degree in Christian education.

On November 18, 1994, Riad was elected general secretary of the Middle East Council of Churches by the General Assembly and in January 1995 he assumed these responsibilities from his predecessor, Mr. Gabriel Habib (who had served as its general secretary from its founding in 1972). The Middle East Council of Churches presently includes three families of churches: the Eastern Orthodox churches (Greek Orthodox), the Oriental Orthodox churches (Armenian, Coptic, and Syrian) and the Protestant churches (Reformed and Episcopal). In the short space of the past four years Mr. Jarjour's leadership in the council has provided some significant accomplishments.

He has brought the Middle East Council's program closer to the grassroots of member churches, rationalized its structure, improved staff interaction and morale, and maintained the council's effective ministry at a time when financial resources have been shrinking. He worked toward giving fuller features to and strengthening the ecumenical ministry of the council to member churches in the Holy Land.

Under his leadership the council has taken a prominent role in fostering Muslim-Christian cooperation in the region. He has been tireless in supporting the cause of the Palestinian people and strengthening the ability of the council to interpret their needs and aspirations to a world audience.

A significant historical moment occurred when the council approved the membership of the Holy Apostolic Catholic Assyrian Church of the East in November 1995, signifying the end of centuries of isolation. This is but one illustration of ecumenical reconciliation that has taken place in recent years.

The council has been able to improve the ability to respond to the region's several crises. The relief work in Iraq has continued to be effective and timely. The council has been able to respond quickly to Iran's latest tragic earthquake. Reconstruction and development work in Lebanon continues to be well targeted and valuable.

Communications have improved remarkably as the council's role as an advocate for the region's vital concerns has became more effective and relationships with ecumenical and international partners strengthened.

Riad himself has become a much sought-after speaker in international circles, effectively interpreting the ecclesiastical, religious, social, and historical situation of the Middle East region.

Meanwhile, Rose has not been silent but has been on the forefront. Her ministry has particularly concentrated on youth and women. In an area where women have culturally been

Riad Jarjour

overlooked and many churches still do not acknowledge their leadership by ordination, Rose has emerged as a very dynamic leader.

In 1983 at the World Council of Churches (WCC) General Assembly in Vancouver, Canada, and again in 1991 in Canberra, Australia, she was elected to the WCC Central Committee. From 1986 to 1993 she served as moderator of the World Council of Churches' Middle East Resource Sharing Group, of which she is still a member.

From 1986 to 1991 she worked diligently with Riad to resuscitate the role and effectiveness of the Fellowship of Middle East Evangelical Churches (FMEEC), concentrating on areas of ministry to youth and women and developing programs for pastors and laity. The FMEEC is an organization that brings together Episcopal, Lutheran, and several Reformed churches of the Middle East. In 1991 she was elected General Secretary of the FMEEC and was unanimously reelected in 1997 to serve a second term. During this period of seven years Rose Jarjour has been able to guide the FMEEC in some new directions, strengthening the mission and ministry of the fellowship and demonstrating the potential effectiveness of such a church body. These include:

- Working to include the Iranian churches, which have endured new realities and limited opportunities in the postrevolutionary period.
- Fostering increased attention to and cooperation with church-related schools throughout the region.
- Inviting the various Protestant churches of the region to a dialogue for unity and drafting a proposal for such unity. This concept has been manifested in true form by FMEEC, thereby increasing cooperation among the churches.
- Organizing seminars to treat topics of Reformed theology, identity, witness, and challenges currently facing the churches of the Middle East. Other topics considered in the seminars are related to the ministry and witness of Evangelical churches for the future and their relationship to their sister churches and to the ecumenical movement.
- Raising the concerns of pastors' wives to the forefront through training and equipping them to be co-ministers. This is especially important in the Middle East where the social context requires a certain role for the clergy wife, often taking for granted her ability and willingness.
- Encouraging theological education for young women, who have an equally important message and ministry, despite the fact that no church in the region yet ordains women to the ministry.

The significance of the above accomplishments and involvements can only be accredited to a couple who has had and continues to have a deep commitment to God in Jesus Christ and to the ecumenical nature of the Christian church. To visit the Jarjours in Ayia Napa, Limassol, or Lebanon is to be received with Christian embraces illustrative of the warmth with which each goes about doing ministry.

Haydn White was formerly Associate for Global Education and Leadership Development, Presbyterian Church (U.S.A.).

Yong-Bock Kim: A Man of Many Dreams

by Daniel J. Adams and Carol Chou Adams

In 1979 during the military regime of Park Chung-Hee, Yong-Bock Kim and other leading dissident figures received an invitation to attend a wedding. It was planned as an opportunity for the dissident community to gather, since all meetings were forbidden by the government. Kim was looking forward to attending, for it would be a time to renew friendships, share information, and consider the prospects for the future. It would also be a time to relax and enjoy a brief respite from the political tensions gripping Seoul and the entire nation of Korea. As he left his home in northern Seoul to attend the wedding, he was filled with anticipation. That evening, when he failed to return home, Kim's wife, Marion, sensed that something was terribly wrong. She immediately began phoning the homes of others who had been invited to the wedding only to discover that they, too, had failed to return home. It soon became apparent that the intelligence services had discovered the true nature of this "wedding" and had broken in and rounded up the country's leading dissident figures in one swoop.

The next several weeks were filled with uncertainty. Where was Yong-Bock Kim? Two weeks passed, and then slowly the wedding guests began to reappear with tales of interrogation and torture. One man told of hearing Kim's voice in the next room at a secret interrogation center. His family heaved sighs of relief, believing that at least he was alive. Finally, after considerable effort, Kim was located and eventually freed. He had been tortured and suffered from severe injuries to his spine, and there were fears that the injuries might be permanent. With treatment and a period of rest, however, he was able to recover his health.

Who is Yong-Bock Kim, and why is it that the officials of the military government would take such an interest in him? Kim was born in 1938 in North Cholla Province in southwest Korea during a time of great national suffering due to the colonization of the country by the Japanese. His father, who worked under the Japanese in Manchuria, died as a result of the hardships he suffered, leaving his mother to support the family as best she could.

Thus, from an early age, Kim became aware of the suffering of the common people of Korea, the masses who seemed to be powerless in the face of foreign colonization, war and ideological oppression, grinding poverty, lack of educational opportunity, and continuing military control over virtually every aspect of cultural and national life.

Kim was fortunate to be able to study at Seoul's prestigious Yonsei University, a school founded by American Presbyterian missionaries. In 1960 following the student revolution that toppled the regime of Syngman Rhee, Kim was arrested for taking part in the student movement and spent several months in prison. After graduating from Yonsei, he came to the United States and completed his education at Princeton Theological Seminary, receiving an MDiv degree in 1966 and a PhD in 1976.

Yong-Bock Kim

When Yong-Bock returned to Korea, he joined a number of other pastors and theologians to engage in theological reflection concerning the events taking place in the country. Out of this process of ongoing reflection a new theological movement came into being—*minjung* theology—focusing on the suffering of the masses and their struggle for social and economic justice. One of the most significant contributions to *minjung* theology is Kim's emphasis upon social biography, whereby social and cultural history is reinterpreted and rewritten from the point of view of the *minjung* (the people). Taken together with the resources of scripture, social biography forms one of the integral elements of *minjung* theology today.

A tireless ecumenist, Yong-Bock has served at one time or another on committees of virtually all of the well-known ecumenical agencies, such as the World Council of Churches, the World Alliance of Reformed Churches, the Christian Conference of Asia, and the Korean National Council of Churches. Kim was recently elected moderator of the department of theology of the World Alliance of Reformed Churches (WARC) at its 1997 general council meeting in Debrecen, Hungary. Along with the Taiwanese theologian C. S.

Song, the president of WARC, Kim is pushing for a serious theological consideration of economic justice. Indeed Kim's recent lectures and essays are focused on the issue of global economic justice and an appropriate Christian response.

Asian theology and theological education remain at the heart of Kim's life and work. In mid-1997 he and Feliciano Cariño of the Philippines, in cooperation with a committee of theologians drawn from all over Asia, convened the first Congress of Asian Theologians at a church conference center south of Seoul. Initial interest in the Congress was so high that scores of applicants had to be turned away, and many from Korea were unable to be housed at the conference site. *This Congress of Asian Theologians was the first time that so many Asian theologians had been together in one place and at one time*. There was excitement in the air as theologians from all over Asia began to forge an identity and an awareness that they will be leading the church into the third millennium. Plans are now underway for the second Congress of Asian Theologians to be held in India in 1999.

Where is Yong-Bock Kim today? Well, he may be in Hong Kong, or Geneva, or London, or Bangalore, or perhaps New York, meeting with church officials, sharing with ecumenical leaders, planning with Asian theologians, or speaking to a group of theological students. Or, you may find him in his office at Hanil University and Presbyterian Theological Seminary, where he serves as president. Hanil, founded as a Bible school for women by American Presbyterian missionaries seventy-five years ago, is now a fully accredited university with both undergraduate and graduate programs. One of these programs, the Asia Pacific Graduate School of Theological Studies, was founded by Kim as an international graduate school for the training of church leaders from Asia and around the world. Students from over ten countries have studied in this unique program, and it is rapidly emerging as a center for global theological education in Asia.

Supporters and critics alike refer to Kim as a dreamer. As a youth from rural North Cholla Province he *dreamed* of attending university in Seoul. As a university student he *dreamed* of a more democratic Korea and of going to the United States for graduate study. When he returned to Korea in 1976 with a Princeton doctorate in hand, he *dreamed* of a Korea where justice would prevail. As he forged the beginnings of *minjung* theology on the anvil of persecution and imprisonment, he *dreamed* of a time when the voice of the poor and oppressed would be heard. At Hanil University and Presbyterian Theological Seminary, he *dreamed* of remaking a small local Bible school into a major university. Through the Asia Pacific Graduate School of Theological Studies, he *dreamed* of a place where Asian church leaders could study theology in their own cultural context using their own categories of thought and hold their heads high in a theological world long dominated by the West.

Yong-Bock Kim is still dreaming, and his dreams have come true, at least in part, because of the International Leadership Development Program of the Presbyterian Church (U.S.A.). In fulfilling his dreams, he is making it possible for the dreams of countless others in Asia to become a reality!

Daniel J. Adams is a mission worker and professor of theology at Hanil University and Presbyterian Theological Seminary in Chonju, Korea.

Carol Chou Adams, a native of Taiwan, is Professor of Christian Education at Hanil University and Presbyterian Theological Seminary in Chonju, Korea.

[Another of Kim's important contributions is the role that he has played and continues to play in making the insights of Korean theology known to the English-speaking world. In 1981 Kim edited a collection of essays entitled *Minjung Theology: People as the Subjects of History*. The first edition was published under Kim's name as editor, but it was banned by the military government and circulated in Korea only in photocopied editions bound in an unmarked cover. In order to make the work more readily available in Asia, it was reissued in 1983 under the editorship of the Commission of Theological Concerns of the Christian Conference of Asia, and it continues to be one of the best introductions to *minjung* theology available in English. Kim's second major English work is *Messiah and Minjung: Christ's Solidarity with the People for New Life*, first published in Hong Kong in 1992 and now available on the Internet. Most of Kim's more recent writings are available on the Internet at <http://ccas.peacenet.or.kr>. Kim's ability to communicate in several languages has enabled him to become one of the most well-known spokespersons for the *minjung* theology movement.]

I-to Loh: Finding Asia's Cultural Voice in the Worship of God

by Don A. Pittman

One of the most internationally recognized leaders among contemporary Asian Christians, I-to Loh currently serves as president and professor of worship, church music, and ethnomusicology at Tainan Theological College and Seminary, Tainan, Taiwan. His unique vocation in Christian ministry has been the preservation and promotion of Asian music and hymnody for the global church. Throughout his distinguished career as a teacher, hymnologist, and ethnomusicologist, he has been an advocate for theological contextualization and liturgical inculturation in Asia, while at the same time making musical resources from Asia and other parts of the world available for the worship enrichment of the broader ecumenical church.

Born in Taiwan in 1936 during the island's fifty-year period of Japanese colonization (1895–1945), Loh's interest in indigenous Asian music began at a very early age. His father was a highly respected minister of the Presbyterian Church in Taiwan (PCT) who served for more than twenty years as a missionary among various aboriginal tribes of the island. The ancestors of the Puyuma, Ami, Paiwan, Rukai, and Yami peoples with whom he worked, lived in Taiwan thousands of years before Han Chinese from the mainland began migrating there in significant numbers. As a young boy inspired by his father's ministry, Loh came not only to appreciate the traditional music of the indigenous people of Taiwan but to understand the role of music in the maintenance of their cultural identity in the face of Han Chinese dominance and Japanese occupation.

Loh's ministerial vocation has also been shaped by the persistent and prophetic witness of the Presbyterian Church in Taiwan for peace, social justice, and self-determination. When the Japanese military government left the island at the end of World War II, it was immediately replaced by that of

Chiang Kai-shek's Kuomintang (KMT) from China, which imposed on the local people a harsh rule of martial law that was not lifted until 1987. Throughout the period of martial law, even at the cost of constant harassment and the disappearance, imprisonment, and exile of numerous church leaders, the PCT continued to speak out to promote human rights and democratic freedoms. As a student at Tainan Theological College and Seminary, the island's oldest church-related institution of higher education and a center of Taiwanese nationalism, Loh was greatly influenced by the faculty's special concerns to examine the relationship between Christianity and culture and to set forth contextual theologies. In this regard, he was especially tutored by the well-known minister, scholar, and ecumenist, Shoki Coe, who served as the school's first Taiwanese president from 1949 until 1965.

After receiving his master of divinity degree from Tainan, Loh went abroad for advanced studies in church music. After receiving a master of sacred music degree in 1966 from Union Theological Seminary in New York, and after another year of advanced study developing new compositional skills, he returned to his alma mater in southern Taiwan to teach church music and direct the school's growing music program. His own research interests in indigenous music were encouraged by a special assignment during 1969 to 1972 by the Urban Rural Mission Committee of the Christian Conference of Asia

I-to Loh

(CCA) to collect Asian songs, some of which were published in his first major publication, *New Songs of Asian Cities* (CCA, 1972). In addition to teaching in Tainan during the 1972–1973 academic year, he also served part-time at Tunghai University in Taichung, Taiwan, as the coordinator for the Research Center for the Study of Taiwanese Music and, beginning in 1973, editor of the *Tunghai Ethnomusicological Journal*. These appointments provided further opportunities for recording and studying the music of his homeland. After completing a program of doctoral studies in the United States in 1982, he received a PhD degree in music, with a major in ethnomusicology, from the University of California at Los Angeles.

Upon receipt of the degree, he was commissioned as a missionary by the General Board of Global Ministries of the United Methodist Church for a teaching ministry at the Asian Institute for Liturgy and Music (AILM) in Manila, the Philippines. Between 1982 and 1994, Loh served as an important member of its music faculty, while also traveling frequently to Taiwan, where he continued to teach part-time in Tainan as well as in Taipei at Taiwan Theological College and Seminary. At the same time, he was becoming increasingly active in various professional associations and in ecumenical church work. For example, he was a charter member of the World Association for Chinese Church Music (1972), serving as its general secretary for a number of years. He was a music adviser for the Sixth General Assembly of the World Council of Churches (WCC) in Vancouver in 1983, the Seventh General Assembly in Canberra in 1991, and the WCC consultation on Justice, Peace, and the Integrity of Creation in Seoul in 1989. He served as the music director for the 1985, 1990, and 1995 General Assemblies of the CCA, and its 1989 and 1994 Asian Mission Conferences. Since 1984, he has served on the teaching team of Ecumenical Seminars on Liturgy and Music in Denmark, Zimbabwe, the Philippines, Costa Rica, Australia, San Lucia, Switzerland, and Taiwan. In 1994 he chose to leave his position at AILM in Manila and returned to full-time teaching at Tainan Theological College and Seminary, where he also became chair of the Department of Church Music and in 1995 the school's eighth president.

Central to Loh's life and work has been his aim to help Asian Christians find their own cultural voice in the worship of God. He has sought to affirm the unique gifts and talents that God has given to all peoples and to oppose efforts to restrict authentic Christian expression to forms once transmitted to Asia by Western missionaries. As he once remarked,

> Fascinated by the new Christian faith and associating it with the "advanced" Western culture (technology, in particular), Asian converts have probably idealized and absolutized these Christian expressions and values. To the new converts it seemed necessary to denounce their past and to remove the association of pagan practices in order to prove their true conversion to Christ. Unfortunately, it led to a denial of the native culture and values; Christians became alienated from their local culture and their own people. They were eager to learn and adapt the new Christian expression, including

liturgies and music. Eventually, they became so attached to these forms that they regarded them as the absolutely authentic way of Christian expression.

As a corrective to this limiting development, Loh has sought to help Asians reclaim aspects of their indigenous cultures in order to enrich forms of Christian worship not only in Asia but throughout the world.

I-to Loh has published more than twenty books and collections of songs, many with recordings, which he has authored, compiled, and edited. One of them, *Sound the Bamboo,* is the official hymnal of the Christian Conference of Asia and is widely used in churches around the world. Most of the 280 hymns, in 38 languages and from 22 Asian countries, exhibit indigenous styles. Another, *All Peoples Praise,* includes more than 100 hymns, liturgical responses, and anthems. The author of more than a dozen scholarly papers on contextual music and worship, Loh was named a Fellow of the Hymn Society of America in 1995, the first person outside of the United States, Canada, and western Europe to receive this tribute.

Don A. Pittman is Associate Professor of the History of Religions and Chair, Department of Theological Studies at Tainan Theological College and Seminary, Taiwan.

"There is no program that has built a greater reservoir of goodwill in the relations of our church than Leadership Development with its extremely significant framework for the cooperation between our church and related churches overseas. The overseas scholars are the gifts of other churches through the presence here of persons who have returned to become the most significant leaders of the church in this generation."

Newton Thurber, former area liaison for South Asia/China/Hong Kong/Taiwan, for the Presbyterian Church (U.S.A.)

Pierre Shamba Manenga:
Conciliator and Dedicated Churchman

by Virginia Pruitt

I grew up in a little village in the Congo forest," Pierre Shamba Manenga used to reply when, as a student in the United States on a PC(USA) Leadership Development grant he was asked about his background. That "little village" in the Bakuba Kingdom of Central Africa was an outpost of one of the eleven mission stations of the American Presbyterian Congo Mission. That Shamba and a number of other outstanding leaders in the new nation and the new church would emerge from that village was due to good genes, smart minds, and a solid Christian education provided through the mission church and schools.

Shamba pursued his education through the mission school system, graduating from its top-notch, university-preparatory secondary school and then being awarded a scholarship for college in the United States. He first briefly attended Stillman College in Tuscaloosa, Alabama, improving his use of English, for all his studies until then had been in French, the official language of the Congo as a colony of Belgium. Proficiency in both French and English was one of Shamba's accomplishments.

At Austin College in Sherman, Texas, a Presbyterian-affiliated institution from which he graduated in 1964, this young African was the first black student to live on campus. Warmly welcomed by other students and the faculty, and received into the fellowship and membership of the campus church, still he sometimes met with hurtful discrimination in the town. He sang in the college choir but was not permitted to go along on choir tours lest his presence create awkward situations in housing. He did not let such treatment cause bitterness. On a return visit to the college years later Shamba was honored and commended by faculty who had known him in those earlier days for the gentle, gracious manner with which he had succeeded in integrating that southern campus, thenceforth freely and cordially incorporating blacks into all activities.

Upon his return to the Congo, Shamba was made "directeur" of the secondary school he had previously attended. Formerly he had been one of my pupils. Now he was my principal, a very able and admirable one indeed. This was the missionary experience in those transitional years when local leadership, having completed the mission's courses of training and preparation, was now assuming the administration of the institutions of preaching, teaching, and healing, no longer under an America-based mission but supervised by the Eglise Presbyterienne au Congo (EPC).

Shamba married Becky, his beloved, supportive helpmate, after which he received yet another scholarship for advanced study in the United States. This time Becky was with him, sharing in the American experience as he earned a postgraduate degree from Howard University in Washington, D.C.

Through the chaotic years in which the Congo struggled from colonial status to independence, the churches—Protestant and Catholic—proved to be a strategic stabilizing force. During this difficult period Pierre Shamba Manenga played a significant leadership role, *Pierre Shamba and Becky Manenga* serving two consecutive terms as moderator of the General Assembly of the Congo Presbyterian Church.

In recent years Shamba has occupied the position of administrator at the Good Shepherd Hospital located in the outskirts of Kananga, capital of the Kasai Province. This is the only hospital ministering in a vast area of need, extending its medical care through a system of outlying clinics staffed by graduates of the hospital's nurses' training school. Shamba's particular function there is in public relations mediating between the church's hospital and the government's givers, between "town" and "gown." His remarkable gifts as a conciliator continue to make a valued contribution in maintaining Good Shepherd Hospital as a viable working institution through many critical ups and downs, financial and political.

Pierre Shamba Manenga, dedicated and outstanding churchman, continues in leadership in the Presbyterian Church in the Congo and has also represented that church in official exchange visitations to partner churches in the United States. He continues, too, as a warm and close friend. He was best man in our son's wedding in 1963 and today vacations in our old vacation house in Congo.

He and Becky have three children. Cecile, the eldest and the only daughter, is married to an American and lives in Texas. Of the two sons, one teaches in the recently established Protestant University in Kinshasa, the Congo capital, and the other is in medical school in the Ivory Coast expecting to return as a qualified doctor to the Good Shepherd Hospital.

Virginia Pruitt is a former mission worker in the Congo.

Maake Masango:
A One-Person Committee on Ministry

by Marvin Simmers

O n a beautiful Sunday morning in 1979, when our Hillside Presbyterian congregation in Decatur, Georgia, had moments for "Passing the Peace of Christ," I turned around and greeted a new couple and their daughter. Immediately when they spoke, I realized that they were not native Georgians, or United States southerners, for that matter. They were from the south, however—South Africa. At that moment I met Maake, Pauline, and six-year-old Tshepo Masango. Maake was beginning his master of theology studies at Columbia Theological Seminary, and the family had chosen Hillside as their church home. Since that meeting I have treasured, and my life has been enriched by, my friendship with the Masango family.

Though not of imposing physical stature, Maake is a giant in many ways. His quiet manner and genuine humility requires one to discover from other sources the many ways in which one man's ministry has touched so many in profound ways in the life of the church in South Africa, North America, and around the world.

Maake served as a pastor in the Presbyterian Church of South Africa from 1975 until 1979, when he came to Columbia Theological Seminary. During those years, and prior to that in his years as a seminary student, Maake was heavily involved in ecumenical activities that included a Student Christian Movement Conference in Lesotho. He attended conferences in Kenya, Sudan, Cyprus, Egypt, and Syria at the invitation of the World Council of Churches to participate in dialogues between Christians and Muslims. Maake also organized and led an educational tour to the Holy Land, Greece, and Rome for clergy and their spouses.

Maake's boundless energy, keen mind, and deep commitment allow him to focus on many things at one time, and do all of them well. While pursuing his studies at Columbia Seminary, and later at the Presbyterian School of

Christian Education, Maake also served congregations in Atlanta, Georgia, and Richmond, Virginia. A dynamic speaker and gifted interpreter of scripture, Maake was in great demand as a preacher. In 1982, just before his return to South Africa, Maake was the main preacher at the Global Mission Conference of the Presbyterian Church in the United States.

From 1982 to 1987 Maake and Pauline were back in South Africa, where Maake was the director of his denomination's Department of Christian Education (Tshepo remained in the United States to continue her education). He traveled extensively throughout Africa, conducting teacher and officer training workshops and speaking at conferences. He also visited the United States as a member of a six-week exchange program between the Presbyterian Church (U.S.A.) and the Presbyterian Church in South Africa. During that time he conducted worship and preached in twelve different states.

Maake Masango

In 1985 when tensions in South Africa were running high because of apartheid, Maake was one of the few Presbyterian Church of South Africa clergy to sign the Kairos Document, a faith statement similar to the Declaration of Barmen. This is all the more remarkable because at that time the membership of the denomination was white by a large majority.

Maake and Pauline returned to Atlanta and Hillside in 1987, much to the great joy of the congregation, and he began his doctoral program at Columbia Seminary in pastoral counseling. It didn't take long for the word to get around—Maake's back!

A great favorite with youth, Maake was one of the 1989 Montreat Youth Conference preachers and made a deep and lasting impression on the thousand or so youth and adults who were in attendance. In July 1992 more than 6,000 youth and their adult leaders gathered at Purdue for the Youth Triennium. The theme that year was "Through the Waters," and we were fortunate to have Maake as one of the morning preachers. His gentle spirit, powerful preaching, and unrelenting pursuit of justice in the midst of the battles to overcome apartheid in South Africa came through in that sermon. It was truly one of the moving experiences of the Triennium.

In spite of the pressures of his studies, Maake led workshops in a number of presbyteries. He also traveled to the West Indies, where he was the preacher on the occasion of the celebration of the Centennial of the Moravian Church in St. Thomas and St. Croix.

Upon completing his doctoral work in 1994, Maake and Pauline returned to South Africa (Tshepo continued her studies in the United States). Maake accepted a call to serve as a pastoral counselor to pastors and congregations and to take the lead in cross-cultural ministry and church growth efforts. He was, as one person put it, "a sort of one-person Committee on Ministry."

The year 1996 was even busier than usual for Maake. He was appointed pastor of St. Giles Presbyterian Church, the first black pastor of a white congregation in Sandringham, a wealthy suburb of Johannesburg. Maake was also elected moderator designate of the General Assembly of the Presbyterian Church in South Africa for 1996–1997. In the fall of 1996 Maake was again in the United States, where he spent almost a month itinerating in Presbyterian churches as one of the International Peacemakers for the Presbyterian Church (U.S.A.) Peacemaking Program.

Several years ago, I had the privilege of attending a conference in which Dr. James Forbes delivered a major address. His central message that day was that the most important ministry the church could be about in our day is the ministry of healing. Families and individuals feel the stress of alienation, congregations and denominations are suffering from the wounds inflicted by ideologies, nations are torn internally by cultural strife, wars continue to spring up between nations. When I reflect on Dr. Forbes's call for the church to be engaged in healing ministry, one of the premier healers that comes to mind is Maake Masango. In a recent interview Maake said, "In South Africa today we are called to heal the past, to heal the wounds caused by the brutality of the past, and then to send out those who have been healed to be the healers." At this moment, there is no greater calling for the church on any continent. The church and the world would be blessed if there were more Maake Masangos.

Marvin Simmers is Coordinator of the Pastor, Educator, and Lay Leader Support Program Team in the Christian Education Program Area of the Congregation Ministries Division, PC(USA).

Mary Mikhael:
Partner in Education and Advocacy

by Mary Mikhael

[Dr. Mary Mikhael, a former International Leadership Development scholar, is an excellent example of partnership in mission. This partnership embodies faithfulness and witness, solidarity and mutuality, support and prayer, education and advocacy. Many images and words come to mind in describing Dr. Mikhael: a dedicated follower of Christ, a strong advocate for women, an affirming educator, a gentle spirit, a heartwarming smile, a welcoming presence, a challenging ministry, and most of all, an inspiring example of faithfulness.

Dr. Mikhael now serves as the president of the Near East School of Theology (NEST) in Beirut, Lebanon. NEST is an interdenominational Protestant theological seminary serving the Evangelical churches of the Middle East and some African churches. As a member of the Synod of Syria and Lebanon, Mary, a lay Christian educator, serves the church in many capacities. As a partner of the Presbyterian Church (U.S.A.), she helps Presbyterians and other American Christians to strengthen their historic ties with the church in the Middle East. The following is a personal reflection written by Mary about her journey of partnership with the Presbyterian Church (U.S.A.)—*Roula Alkhouri, a native of Syria, is a Leadership Development Scholar and former Consultant on Women and Leadership Development, Office of Global Education and International Leadership Development, Worldwide Ministries Division, PC(USA).*]

THE PRESBYTERIAN CHURCH (U.S.A.) AND I

Being a student in the Near East School of Theology (NEST) in the seventies put me in direct touch with the PC(USA) through professors who helped shape my personality as a Presbyterian Christian. To Dr. Kenneth Bailey, the Rev. Else Farr, Mrs. Carol Weir, and many others, I give my warmest regards and my sincere gratitude.

In the mid-1970s, I was teaching in a school for blind people while studying at NEST. Those were the first years of the Lebanese civil war when many young people lost their sight because of all the violence that took place. I had the responsibility of rehabilitating and training them to adapt to their new situation. The physical and emotional intensity of my work left me exhausted and depressed. My teacher Carol Weir, a missionary from the Presbyterian Church, suggested that I go to the United States for the final year of my master's program. She initiated the conversation with the Presbyterian School of Christian Education (PSCE) in Richmond, Virginia. I was accepted at PSCE for the school year of 1981 to 1982. This was my first year ever as a university student able to devote all my time to school work, not having to worry about a full-time job.

At PSCE I experienced a mixture of feelings. It was fun to spend long hours in the library and to be exposed to a wide variety of Christian education approaches. My Presbyterianism was nurtured and my relatedness to the PC(USA) grew firmer. However, my heart was always heavy because those were hard days for Lebanon.

After completing my degree, I moved to Stony Point Presbyterian Conference Center in New York on a two-month mission assignment. This was the first step into a new beginning in my life and career. At that point, I had already signed a contract with NEST to join the faculty and was on my way back to Beirut. However, those were the months of the Israeli invasion of Lebanon, when Beirut was bombarded as never before. West Beirut was surrounded, and the Palestinian refugees were to be evacuated. NEST was converted temporarily to a

Mary Mikhael

Palestinian hospital that was relocated because of Israeli attacks. The future of Beirut was on the devil's palm, as the Arabic proverb goes. In those horrifying months, I could not have been in a safer place than the Stony Point Center with the care and love of the Presbyterians at 475 Riverside Drive. To all those who worked in the units of mission, women, and education, I express deep gratitude for holding me in those hard days and for making me feel like a family member. I found a great deal of support for my future educational needs from Dr. Paul Hopkins, the Rev. Haydn White, and the late Dr. Esther Stine. Dr. Stine herself carried my application forms to Teachers College at Columbia University and insisted that the deadline for application should be overlooked in my case. Thus, I started my studies at Columbia in September 1982.

The great challenge I faced at Columbia was completing my studies as quickly as possible in order to be ready to go back to NEST. Because of the political situation most of the non-Lebanese faculty departed, leaving NEST in a desperate situation. Therefore, the support of the Presbyterian Church (U.S.A.) meant a lot more than mere financial backing. Had it not been for that support, I would not have been able to dedicate my time and energy to my studies while waiting for the Lebanese war to ease and for NEST to resume its programs.

Being in New York City and studying at Columbia University and Union Theological Seminary was a compelling and enlightening experience. However, being related to the PC(USA) offices at 475 Riverside Drive, to the Stony Point Center, and to the folks who lived in the Morningside Gardens played an even greater role in helping me become what I am today. In fact, in New York, and particularly at Stony Point Center, my awareness of world issues was developed. Even though the Middle Eastern issues lay heavy on my heart, I came to understand those many nations around the world who struggle for social justice and other human rights and suffer other kinds of oppression. Had it not been for my experience and education at Stony Point, many nations and countries would have remained just like dots of different sizes on the world map.

As I went back to Beirut and started teaching at NEST, I found a place to grow and mature in understanding my ministry as a Christian educator and as a Christian woman. In addition to teaching full-time at NEST, I had the opportunity to direct the woman's program of the Middle East Council of Churches (MECC). This maybe was the greatest challenge I had ever faced. The MECC responsibility meant that I worked with local church leaders and national, regional, and international women's groups. This also coincided with the launching of the Ecumenical Decade of Churches in Solidarity with Women. By becoming deeply involved in women's issues, I experienced their pain, their struggles for claiming their identity, and their rights for equal opportunities. As a Christian woman who had the chance to get higher education and to participate in positions of leadership, I realized how many women have been denied both education and leadership, not only in the Middle East but all over the world. However, because of our political situation in the Middle East and our struggle against the Israeli occupation and oppression, our women have had to bear a double dose of pain. Women in the Middle East are caught in violence that they did not initiate. They also suffer a terror over which they have no control.

Between doing theology at the seminary and working with women, my life has been enriched beyond what I deserved or even expected. Because of the PC(USA), I was ready and prepared to encounter many issues related to situations of human pain and struggle.

During the last four years, my journey with the PC(USA) has taken a new turn. Since I started my ministry as the president of NEST, I have felt a strong support from the PC(USA). I do not believe that NEST can or should continue its ministry unless its partnership with the PC(USA) continues to be strengthened. I hope that we will continue to work together as partners with a common vision for God's mission in the world.

I have appreciation and deep gratitude for the PC(USA) that helped me become who I am and also for working with me as a colleague, friend, and partner. Being educated by the PC(USA) is like being grafted onto a wonderful tree that continues to bear fruits. Many thanks!

Mary Mikhael is President of the Near East School of Theology.

Sincere appreciation and deep gratitude to the PC(USA) for helping me become who I am and also for working with me as a colleague, friend, and partner. Being educated by the PC(USA) is like being grafted onto a wonderful tree that continues to bear fruits. Many Thanks!"

Mary Mikhael, President, Near East School of Theology

Mulumba Musumbu Mukundi: His Greatest Gift, His Humility

by Elizabeth D. McAliley

God called Mulumba Musumbu Mukundi and he responded. He was a young man when he took the first steps toward the ministry, when he entered the Preachers' School at Bulape, Congo. He wanted to learn everything he could about God's word, about people, about sharing the good news. His teachers helped him learn how to listen to people in the villages, how to discern their beliefs, and then how to share the gospel from their perspective. His teachers recognized that he had a keen and inquiring mind.

In his journey to answer God's call, he next studied at the School of Theology at Ndesha, Congo. One of his teachers said that he would go to a village with Mulumba Musumbu Mukundi, and within a few minutes he seemed to learn more about the villagers than any of the other students or teachers. He would ask about the beliefs and fears of each person he met on these trips to villages. His teachers also recognized him as a very gifted student. Upon graduation, his professors recommended him for further study in the Protestant Theological Seminary in Yaoundé, Cameroon. There he received a master's degree in both theology and sociology.

Now the time had come for Mulumba to begin his journey as a pastor and a teacher. Thus he returned to the Congo, where he was ordained and became a professor at the School of Theology at Ndesha. He was gentle, yet firm with his students. He taught them how to respond to the needs of the people in culturally appropriate and biblically-based ways. He recognized that as future preachers and church leaders, his students needed to learn how to teach, preach, visit, and live out the realities of the kingdom of God within the culture of the Congo. He became an excellent teacher, leader, and role model.

Soon after his return to the Congo, he married. Few who attended his wedding will forget the events leading up to the ceremony. It was at a time when diesel fuel for the Land Rover was scarce and difficult to find, and his wedding party was a day late starting to the village where his future wife awaited his arrival. It was late on a Saturday afternoon when the wedding party was able to leave and the trip took several hours over wet roads. The Congo night was very dark when the party finally arrived at the village. As is the custom, the party was welcomed with joy and great hospitality. A feast was prepared for the guests. At midnight, with lanterns lit, the whole wedding party and friends proceeded to the small church where the wedding ceremony took place. It was a beautiful night of joy and singing and fellowship. Today Pastor Mulumba is a devoted husband and the father of four children.

Several years later, because of Pastor Mulumba's exceptional intellectual, ethical, and moral leadership, the Presbyterian Community in the Congo (CPC) recommended him for graduate studies in theology in the United States. The Presbyterian Church (U.S.A.) assisted him with scholarship funds that enabled him to earn a master's degree in missiology and a PhD in intercultural studies at Fuller Theological Seminary in Pasadena, California. He and his family readily adapted to the U.S. culture but never forgot their Congo roots and the purpose of his graduate studies. He wanted to better prepare himself and his family to witness and work in the church in Congo. After receiving his doctorate, the Rev. Dr. Mulumba returned to Zaire (now Congo) and again became a professor at the Faculty of Theology (formerly the School of Theology) at Ndesha.

Mulumba Musumbu Mukundi

As one of the few intellectuals in the Kasai, he was pressured by the church and friends to be involved in everything where vision, insight, and moral leadership were important. In 1991 while continuing as a professor at Ndesha, he was elected as the general secretary (stated clerk) of the Presbyterian Community of Zaire (Congo). At the 1998 General Assembly of the Presbyterian Community of Congo, Dr. Mulumba was reelected stated clerk for another eight years. In addition, because of the resignation of the legal representative of the CPC, Dr. Mulumba was asked to serve as interim legal representative.

Because of his love for the kingdom of God and his deep concern for the grassroots of the church, Dr. Mulumba accepted a call to become pastor of a local congregation in a new suburb of Kananga, while maintaining his other responsibilities as teacher, stated clerk, father, and husband. His church is in one of the newer developments in Kananga. Though he is not able to preach every Sunday, he is a pastor who loves his people.

In 1997 the School of Theology became the Presbyterian University of Kananga with Schools of Theology and Sociology. The CPC envisions that eventually the present Christian Medical Institute of the Kasai (IMCK) will become a part of this fledgling university. To give the dynamic, alert, and visionary leadership to this new university venture, Dr. Mulumba was named rector.

One important focus of Dr. Mulumba is partnership with the Presbyterian Church (U.S.A.). To honor the commitment to partnership, in late 1997 for about a month he served a church in Illinois in the Mission to the USA program of the Worldwide Ministries Division of the PC(USA).

As a pastor within the Presbyterian Community Church he is greatly respected for his deep faith, character, insights, wisdom knowledge, and leadership ability. He is firm in challenging his peers and his students to be strong Christian leaders. The Congo is a country in great turmoil and change. As a committed church leader he believes that the church must play a significant role in preparing the people and the country for responsible rule.

Perhaps Dr. Mulumba's greatest gift is his humility. The Presbyterian Church (U.S.A.) is fortunate to know him, to have had a role in his educational process, and to have him as a friend and colleague. Because Dr. Mulumba has been faithful to God's call, the Presbyterian Community of Congo is also blessed with an exceptional leader.

Elizabeth D. McAliley is the former Associate Director for Mutual Mission, Worldwide Ministries Division, PC(USA).

Nyambura J. Njoroge:
The First in Many Roles, a Lonely Walk

by Nyambura J. Njoroge

[Princeton Theological seminary granted Nyambura J. Njoroge a "family" scholarship in 1986 to undertake her PhD studies in African theology and ethics. Because the yearly grant was not sufficient to support a family of four (her husband was also granted a scholarship from Princeton to pursue studies in civil engineering), the PC(USA) agreed to supplement the difference. She graduated cum laude in 1992. They returned to Kenya in May 1992 to their respective employers, the Presbyterian Church of East Africa (PCEA), in her case, and the Nairobi City Council in her husband's. But even before they settled down, Nyambura was offered a position with the World Alliance of Reformed Churches (WARC) in Geneva, Switzerland, to establish the women's desk in September of 1992. And so she began a full-time ecumenical ministry around women's concerns. She tells the story of her journey.—Editor]

My theological studies both in Kenya and the United States have enabled me to carry out my ecumenical ministry and contribute to the ongoing search for authentic African Christianity and theology that is gender sensitive. It has also given me a great desire to advocate for theological education for women, especially in the South, because of the difference it makes when one is theologically trained in all the ministries of the church, ordained or not ordained. In my writings, I have emphasized a theology inclusive of all people and different perspectives. Most important, I have sought to recapture the theology of lamentation that I found lacking in missionary/colonial Christianity planted in Africa. Since the days of slavery, Africa's history and reality have been full of loss, pain, suffering, dehumanization, violence, and senseless death. There is no way that we can continue to ignore this reality in our theology or Christianity.

But that's getting ahead of the story. To go back to the beginning, soon after I went to work for WARC, the executive committee decided to move beyond establishing a women's desk to experiment in building and developing a program of partnership between men and women—the "Program to Affirm,

Challenge, and Transform: Women and Men in Partnership in Church and Society," conveniently called PACT. Lo and behold, the President of WARC, Professor Jane Dempsey Douglass (1990–1997), the first woman to hold that office since 1875 and whom I had come to know only socially on the Princeton Seminary grounds, was asked to be the moderator of PACT. Together with a few members of the Executive Committee, we developed PACT and organized regional consultations on the theme of Partnership in God's Mission. (Copies of the books on these consultations in Africa, Asia and the Pacific, Latin America, and the Middle East are available in the WARC office. The reports on the European, Caribbean, and North American consultations were not published as books but are also available through the office.)

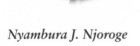

In addition, I was asked to develop a network of women in the Reformed family to ensure that more women are included in all the activities of WARC and other ecumenical bodies. In this regard, one of my greatest challenges was to see that more women from the South attended the twenty-third General Council of WARC, held in Debrecen, Hungary, in August 1997. The original WARC budget did not take into account the fact that without additional financial support, most of the churches in the South could not sponsor women and youth, but only the one delegate (usually a man) who had been included in the budget!

Nyambura J. Njoroge

Other tasks at the twenty-third General Council included coordinating the preparation of the document that was used on "Partnership in God's Mission," one of the three subthemes to be addressed within the broad theme of "Break the Chains of Injustice," and preparing the two-day Women's Pre-Conference in Debrecen. Finally, the General Council decided that PACT had an important task in the life and mission of WARC, and it resolved to create the Department of Partnership of Women and Men of which I am the executive secretary. Cultivating and nurturing partnerships of women and men (*koinonia*) and creating gender awareness and sensitivity in the member churches and in the life and mission of WARC is the primary task ahead of us.

My journey in church and ecumenical ministry, which began in January of

1978 when I joined the seminary in Kenya, has had a major impact on my spiritual and theological encounters as an African woman in several pioneering positions. I was the first woman to join St. Paul's United Theological College in Limuru, Kenya; the first woman to be ordained in the PCEA and in the Kenyan church; the first African woman to study at Louisville Presbyterian Theological Seminary (completing a master's of arts and religion, 1984–1985) and to undertake PhD studies at Princeton; the first African to be employed by WARC; and, while I am still "researching" this, I may be the first African ordained woman to hold a PhD in theological studies. At the moment, I am the only woman of a six-member executive staff, including the general secretary. It is a lonely walk to say the least!

But there have been some challenging—and humbling—experiences, especially since I did not have a role model or conversation partner. True I have met mentors (both men and women) who have not been afraid to hold my hand, despite my own stubbornness. And without the support of my family, both nuclear and extended, I could not have gone very far. My parents have now rested the heavy work. Thanks be to God for their love, care, and commitment. At an early stage, my husband promised my parents his support for my ministry. Thanks be to God again, for he has faithfully done so, to the extent of forfeiting his lucrative career in engineering to join the family in Geneva. Our life in Princeton helped us to grow as partners and that has continued to sustain us even when the going has been very rough! It is this partnership in the home that has given me hope that *koinonia* is possible even when social and cultural constructions of gender/racial discrimination continue to profess otherwise. Living in Princeton and Geneva has also meant that our children have become global nomads, with all the blessings and shortcomings that brings.

Can joy and life come out of sorrow and lamentation, I ask? As I write, it is Holy Week. Maybe that is from whence my answer will come. But I have to do more searching, for the African Rachel continues to lament and bitterly weep for her children that are no more! It is four years since the genocide in Rwanda. Because of my ecumenical ministry my eyes have been opened to the senseless suffering in the world, especially of women and children. So I have joined Rachel, Hanna, Mary, Rizpah and so many others in lamentation and weeping until . . .

Dr. Nyambura J. Njoroge is Executive Secretary, Department of Partnership of Women and Men, World Alliance of Reformed Churches.

Prakai Nontawasee:
Advocate for Women and Children

by June Ramage Rogers

[Large numbers of Thailand's most gifted women have been International Leadership Development Scholars during the last fifty years. Their names are now legend. Among them are Saisuree Chutikul, former minister of youth in Thailand and currently a senator in the parliament and chair of the Committee on Women, Children and the Elderly; Kamol Arayaprateep, the first Thai to receive a PhD in Old Testament; Woranut Pantupong, leader in both Thai and Asian women's concerns, serving at one time as the chair of the Asian Christian Women's Committee; Boon Mee Julkeeree, former director of the Women's Department of the Church of Christ in Thailand—and many, many more! All of these women have served the wider church at innumerable ecumenical gatherings—Editor]

Prakai Nontawasee was ordained as a minister of the Church of Christ in Thailand in 1995. Unlike most, her ordination was not the beginning of ministry but the culmination of years of service to her church, her country, and the world. As early as 1967 she went to study at McCormick Theological Seminary in Chicago, which, as it turned out, was a healing experience spiritually for her. Everyone was friendly and helpful, a contrast to her first year of study overseas at the University of Michigan as a Fulbright Scholar in 1965, where her living situation was not as positive.

Prakai tells a funny story about her first Christmas away from home. A program was arranged by Betty Parkinson for all overseas students under the Presbyterian U.S.A. Mission Board to spend Christmas together at the Stony Point Center in New York. It was a fruitful program, she says, not only because it was so much fun to be together, but because of the insights gained from exposure to ecumenical relationships.

At Stony Point Guest House, gingerbread men were hung at the side of each stair step. Prakai had never seen this kind of "bread" before. "I didn't know what it was," she exclaimed. One day a picture was taken as all the Thai students gathered on the stairs. Some of the gingerbread men were stepped on and broken to pieces. The Thai students were shocked to learn that the gingerbread men were not only Christmas decorations but were to be eaten. Prakai later laughingly remarked, "I confirmed that on that day, I killed three gingerbread men!"

Margaret Flory, former director of the Office of Student World Relations, remarks in her article in *Church and Society*, November/December 1986–January/February 1987, that the experience of the Thai students that day at Stony Point was one of many experiences in which students met each other and later remembered both the sad and the funny aspects of life in the United States. "Such is the stuff," said Margaret, "of which the ecumenical movement is built, as Christ's disciples from many nations meet each other and interact, 'no longer strangers and foreigners but fellow citizens with the saints and members of the household of God' (Eph. 2:19, RSV, alt.)."

Returning to Thailand in 1968, Prakai immediately put to use her newly acquired English skills by teaching English as a second language at Prince Royal's College. She used what she had learned in teaching young elementary students in the United States, where the youngsters had enjoyed her classes.

Her enhanced knowledge of Christian education helped in teaching Sunday School at the First Church of Chiangmai, where she organized a junior church. Her skills were rapidly recognized by the Church of Christ in Thailand, and

Prakai Nontawasee

for the next four years Prakai served as the chairperson of the Christian Education Department of the Church of Christ in Thailand. One of the events that she remembers most was the gathering of a team to write curriculum for teaching ethics to the junior and senior high school classes in mission schools throughout Thailand.

In 1980 McGilvray Theological Seminary had merged with Payap University to become the Faculty of Theology. There Prakai team-taught Christian education with Jane Arp, an American Presbyterian mission worker. Joined by mission workers from New York University and the Christian Church, Disciples of Christ, they strengthened the team, working and sharing their experiences not only in teaching but in their lives. It was an enriching and unforgettable experience for all of them.

Prakai is forthright about the role that the Presbyterian Church (U.S.A.)'s support played in her life's work. "It broadened my vision of the world, deepened my theological perspective, and provided me with an opportunity to be involved in church activities related to women and children. This increased awareness soon led to my being elected as the chairperson of the Women's Organization of the Church of Christ in Thailand and appointed to the International Committee for the World Day of Prayer."

In later years her ministry was almost entirely focused on women's and children's issues. I got to know Prakai well when I was directing the Action Study on Child Prostitution and Tourism for the Ecumenical Coalition for Third World Tourism in Bangkok. When the day came to present the reports of the study teams from the Philippines, Sri Lanka, and Thailand in 1990, and present an interfaith perspective on the issues, there was absolutely no doubt as to who would present the Protestant reflection. In her quiet, but prophetic style, Prakai Nontawasee, then vice moderator of the Church of Christ in Thailand, closed the speech in which she had stated clearly the theological and biblical premises for a just and faithful life with these words: "If we commit ourselves to the ministry of Jesus Christ and his way, then we must drink his cup of suffering together and be in solidarity with those whose rights to live as children of God are being denied." [1]

Living that creed, she has been instrumental in the founding of the Women's Department's New Home, a shelter for young women (largely from the hill tribes) in the north of Thailand who are in danger of being lured into prostitution; the development of the highly successful AIDS ministry in Chiangmai; the founding of ECPAT, the Ecumenical Campaign Against Child Prostitution (now called End Child Prostitution, Child Pornography, and the Trafficking of Children), of which she was the international chairperson until very recently.

Though saddened in 1996 by the loss of her beloved husband, Prakai still continues to teach at Payap University. During the first semester of 1998, she was one of the teachers of the core course, entitled "Society and Gender Issues." In Payap's Faculty of Theology she is at her post teaching Christian education and theology. She is, as well, the assistant pastor of Dharma Prateep Church in her own community. Her membership on the board of the United Board for Christian Higher Education in Asia keeps her involved regionally and internationally.

I count Prakai as a warm and very wise friend who has been a beacon of hope for women and children in her church, in her nation, and in our world, a woman who speaks passionately and compassionately on behalf of their needs and issues.

As to the role that the Leadership Development Program played in her life, she says, "I certainly thank the Presbyterian Church (U.S.A.) for the financial help and all the kind supports to me which I have cherished all through the years of my life. May the Lord bless our tie of fellowship and our mutual services for our Lord, Jesus Christ."

NOTE

1. From her speech "Biblical Justice," published in *Caught in Modern Slavery: Tourism and Child Prostitution in Asia*, the Report and Proceedings of the Chiang Mai Consultation, May 1–5, 1990.

June Ramage Rogers is a former mission associate in Thailand and member of the Pastoral Team of the International Church of Bangkok, and currently Missionary-in-Residence, Office of Global Education, Worldwide Ministries Division, PC(USA).

Janos Pasztor: Pastor, Teacher, Scholar, Missionary, Truth Speaker, Peacemaker

by Bruce F. Gannaway and Ollie Gannaway

When Janos is asked a question involving theological dimensions, one almost always hears this initial response, "To understand this question, one must begin in the thirteenth or fourteenth century." For an American who normally thinks of twenty-five to fifty years as a very long time, it is startling to even consider a multiple-century context for a simple question. But Janos Pasztor never sees anything unusual in this approach. It is the way answers are given in a Hungarian and Eastern European setting.

The easiest way to acquire this kind of historical perspective is to be born into it and proceed from there. Janos was born in Budapest, Hungary, on May 28, 1925, and his first twelve years of education (1931–1943) were in the schools of the Reformed Church in Hungary. With a call to ministry, he spent the next four years in initial theological studies at the Reformed Theological Academy in Budapest.

After two years of study in psychology and history in Pazmany University, Budapest, he set out to broaden his ecumenical understanding. His first exposure to Reformed theology in the English-speaking world was in the Faculties of Divinity in New College, Edinburgh (1947–1948) and in the University of Manchester (1948–1949). He then returned to complete the required theological preparation for ordination in the Reformed Church in Hungary, receiving a master of divinity degree at the Theological Academy in Budapest (1949–1950).

Always a pastor at heart, he was licensed in 1950 and ordained in 1952 in the Daubian Synod of the Reformed Church in Hungary and became the pastor of the St. Andre Reformed Church in the same year. A pastorate of eighteen years in a most difficult period of Hungary's history was his first major contribution in Christ's ministry. Those were the years immediately before and after the Communist takeover of his country. They were crucial for Janos's personal and theological development. In 1956 when the Hungarian rebellion began, he was on a visit to England and in a Bonhoeffer-type decision he immediately returned to Budapest to be with his people during this time. In the exchange of trains at the Hungarian border, Janos was the only passenger going east into Hungary! Everyone else was fleeing to the west. A pastor was being profoundly formed by willingly sharing the suffering of his people.

Janos often remarked that the years that followed were, contrary to much opinion, good years for the church's real growth and survival. Under the Communist rule, the church lost all of its extra privileges:

Judith and Janos Pasztor

its schools and institutions were nationalized, its rather vast land holdings were confiscated, and church activities were confined to church buildings alone. The church was forced to relearn that it must and could live out of the Word of God alone. Church life was once again refocused on the scriptures and the church's responsibility to be faithful to the gospel in its very circumscribed context. Janos wrote, "They did everything in their power to push the church onto the margin of society and make it irrelevant. Their calculations were shrewd, but they did not take into consideration the power of the gospel that kept us in the church alive."

During these critical years of political stress and theological tension, Janos was selected by the United Presbyterian Church in the U.S.A. as one of its global education scholarship recipients. He spent the academic year 1964–1965 in Princeton Theological Seminary and he made many lasting friends in a new Presbyterian-Reformed arena. In later years he reflected that studies at Princeton had an immense impact on his whole life, both in terms of academic studies and of practical church life. He wrote his appreciation in these words, "The dedication of many in the Presbyterian Church to help students of other churches in their theological studies have borne much fruit. All of these benefits were not only for me, but also for those with whom I served—a living example of the unity of the Body of Christ in glorifying God and serving Christ's gospel among the nations." Upon his return to his home country he earned his doctorate in theology in Budapest in 1969.

In 1970 the United Presbyterian Church in the U.S.A. and the Reformed Church in Hungary united in supplying a theological professor for St. Paul's United Theological College in Limuru, Kenya. St. Paul's trained pastors for its four supporting churches: Anglican, Methodist, Reformed, and Presbyterian. The Pasztors and their children were the first missionaries of the Hungarian Reformed Church to the Two-Thirds World in the modern era and they all became wonderful examples of the church's ecumenical richness and faithfulness. They were excited by their new task, the challenge of mission in Africa, the exposure to a new and different cultural context, and the development of relationships with African students and their families. Janos not only taught courses in theology and homiletics but also preached widely across Kenya. He was an excellent teacher in the classroom and his experience in the Hungarian church's conflict was especially helpful to Kenya students, faculty, and church leaders at the time. Countries in Africa were also going through periods of strained church-state relations and Janos spoke with wisdom and compassion of the struggles his church had endured in Hungary.

After six years (1970–1976) of ecumenical adventure in Kenya, he returned to the Reformed Church in Hungary to become the professor of theology at the illustrious Reformed Theological Academy in Debrecen (1976–1987). New political tensions arose within the Hungarian church and Janos once again earned the right to be called "a truth speaker." But there was a price. He was dismissed from Debrecen and American Presbyterian friends helped arrange for him and Judith to spend a sabbatical year (1987–1988) as a visiting scholar at Columbia Theological Seminary in Decatur, Georgia. He returned to Hungary to serve as both a local pastor and Professor of Ecumenical Theology in the Reformed Seminary of Budapest.

Since his studies in Princeton in the mid-sixties, Janos's life has been increasingly bound up with the PC(USA) as missionary, theologian, and visiting scholar (Columbia Seminary, 1987–1988 and 1997–1998; Dubuque Seminary, 1993). Many congregations in the United States remember Janos and Judith from when they were 1991 International Peacemakers of the PC(USA) speaking throughout the church. Janos was honored by Princeton in 1992 by being invited to deliver the Warfield Lectures.

Pastor, teacher, scholar, churchman, husband, father, missionary, truth speaker, author, peacemaker, friend: each title is important, yet one wonders what is the right order. Each of his friends might arrange them differently. Theological students in Hungary, Kenya, Austria, Romania, and the United

States might suggest a different order, but surely all would avow his impact on their own lives and theological growth. One's own faith and courage revive when remembering the life and ministry of this one of God's servants, Janos Pasztor. And those of us who know him can only think of Janos and Judith Pasztor together, for what is the one without the other?

Bruce F. Gannaway is a former mission worker in Africa and former Associate Director, Partnership in Mission, Worldwide Ministries Division, PC(USA).
Ollie Gannaway, a former mission worker in Africa, was a former associate in the Peacemaking Program, PC(USA).

"The dedication of many in the Presbyterian Church (U.S.A.) to help students of other churches in their theological studies has borne much fruit. All of these benefits were not only for me, but also for those with whom I served—a living example of the unity of the body of Christ in glorifying God and serving Christ's gospel among the nations."

Janos Pasztor, Professor of Theology, Hungary; former mission co-worker in Kenya

---

Manuel Jesús Poblete: Making Theological Education a Reality for the Poor

by Mary Blanche Wortham and George Wortham

I n the depths of the forests of Southern Chile stands the majestic Araucaria pine tree. Many of these trees have stood in these ancient forests for more than 1,000 years. They stand amid other native trees, and the pine nuts they produce are the main staple for the indigenous populations of Southern Chile. When Manuel Jesús Poblete speaks of his ministry and education, he uses the Chilean forest as his image. The trees that feed the people did not come into being overnight. They developed slowly, reaching their maturity with time. So it has been with Manuel. For eighteen years he has worked with the Evangelical Theological Community in the area of theological education by extension. It has been his ministry to bring theological education to the remote parts of Chile. For more than a decade he has worked with the poorest of the poor and helped to raise their educational level. The majority of these folk are Pentecostal and the highest concentration of this church exists in Southern Chile. As a member of one of the three largest Pentecostal churches in Chile, Manuel has had access to this grassroots movement that has been spreading across Chile.

Like the native tree in the forests of the South, Manuel has been learning and maturing for eighteen years. And as Manuel states, this is not possible without the air, sun, rain, and good soil. The tree needs nutrients in order to grow. In recent years it has been the Presbyterian Church (U.S.A.) that has provided those needed nutrients. The scholarship that the church provided for Manuel has given him the opportunity to consolidate eighteen years of practice and learning. It has allowed him to deepen his understanding and explore new possibilities in educational theory. By the end of 1998 he will have completed his studies and will receive a master's degree in curriculum design from the University of Concepción.

But the Araucaria pine does not stand alone. Manuel understands that the tree is an integral part of a forest, of an ecosystem. That is to say, the lone tree cannot grow and develop in isolation. It needs the forest. The saying, "It takes a village to raise a child," rings true in the development of Chilean church leaders and professionals. In the case of Manuel Jesús Poblete, it not only takes a village but also a devoted family and spouse, and folk who work with him on a daily basis. Primary among this support group has been the Evangelical Presbyterian Church in Chile, a partner church with the PC(USA), which supported him and promoted his scholarship. In the Chilean setting, individuals are valued for what they can offer in ser-

vice to the community. Therefore, it is not easy to describe Manuel Jesús Poblete without referring to the proverbial phrase, "You are what your group makes you," and taking into account the group. Or as Manuel says, "You cannot separate the tree from the forest that protects it and supports it."

The Evangelical Presbyterian Church (EPC) in Chile is one of the founding members of the Evangelical Theological Community and has been the primary leader in the development of theological education in Chile. Leaders of the EPC have encouraged their church to support Manuel's abilities and value his contribution to the seminary and to the Protestant and Pentecostal churches in

Manuel Jesús Poblete

Southern Chile. Because of their faith in Manuel, the PC(USA) was encouraged to offer funding and resources for his continued studies. Since 1995 our church in the United States has provided funding, tools, and resources such as a computer to Manuel. To support Manuel to such an extent is no minor commitment by the Evangelical Presbyterian Church, which is extremely poor and limited in its own resources. It is truly an act of grace and a sign of the ecumenical commitment of the Evangelical Presbyterian Church that they would place their trust in Manuel and share its blessings with a Pentecostal brother in a context of great need.

To continue with the image of the Araucaria pine, the Presbyterians in Chile know that the tree that reaches maturity will help feed all the folk who depend on the forest. And so it is with Manuel. The skills that he is receiving will benefit the Presbyterian Church and all the churches in Chile. One concrete example is the challenge of theological education for the next century. The Evangelical Theological Community understands that it needs to reform its educational methods to meet the challenge of rapid change in Latin America. For this reason they have established a work committee called 2001 Curriculum Committee. Manuel Jesús Poblete has been asked to serve on this committee as a professional consultant on curriculum design and in that capacity will design the way in which the Chilean churches will receive theological education in the next century.

Another concrete example relates to the need in the Evangelical Presbyterian Church for a program of study that addresses Presbyterian identity and Reformed theology. The Presbyterians would like to create a two-year program in the northern part of Chile that will combine practice in churches with theological education in confessional studies. Manuel Jesús Poblete has also been asked by the Evangelical Presbyterian Church to be a consultant in the development of this program.

The tasks that lie before Manuel and the churches are not easy ones. These eighteen years of learning and growth have occurred in a time of military dictatorship and continual financial crisis for educational institutions. The challenge to provide theological education is one of the greatest challenges facing the churches in Chile. It is in this context that we must understand the scholarship provided to Manuel Jesús Poblete. In this context, a scholarship is never something given for personal development. It is given for the service of others. And as Manuel has learned from the forests of Southern Chile, time, patience, rain, sun, and good soil will bring to maturity the trees that will feed the people of God.

Mary Blanche Wortham and George Wortham are
mission specialists in Chile.

Rachel Rao: Committed to Women's Rights

by Robert Alter

D uring the summer of 1987 the United States Coast Guard responded to a call for help from a sailing yacht off the coast of Puerto Rico. The yacht was on its way from Massachusetts to St. John's in the Virgin Islands. One of the four passengers on that yacht was suffering from internal bleeding and needed immediate medical attention. A Coast Guard helicopter went to the rescue. The passenger was lifted off the deck of the yacht and taken to a hospital in San Juan. The patient was Rachel Rao, a student from India attending Smith College in Northampton, Massachusetts.

Rachel, who had never been in a boat before, had been invited to spend part of her summer vacation at the end of her second year at Smith accompanying three other women making the trip to St. John's. The Coast Guard authorities contacted Smith College to tell them what had happened. The college sent airline tickets to fly Rachel back to Northampton.

Because of this and other related health problems, the college urged Rachel to take a year off and return to her home in India.

Rachel's father, Sham Rao, a convert to Christianity from Hyderabad in Andra Pradesh, is a Methodist minister with a bachelor of divinity degree from Leonard Theological College of Jabbalpur. Her mother grew up as a Methodist minister's daughter in Karnataka. Though from South India, the Sham Raos began their ministry in the early 1960s by ministering to village congregations in a Hindi-speaking area of Madhya Pradesh. Their three children, Peter, Andrew, and Rachel, were born to them at that time. Later, Rachel's father returned to seminary where he earned a master's degree in theology. While there, he and Rachel's mother accepted an invitation to join the Ecumenical Institute in Chicago and left their children with friends in Bombay. It was a difficult separation, so the Sham Raos decided to leave the institute and return to India two years later.

Rachel's father was then invited to teach theology at Leonard Theological College, which he did for several years. In 1976, the family moved to Rajpur, a suburb of the city of Dehra Dun at the base of the first range of the Himalayan mountains north of New Delhi. Rachel's father became the director of the Christian Retreat and Study Center located there. The two younger children, Andrew and Rachel, were enrolled at Woodstock School, a Christian international boarding school located in Mussoorie in the hills above Rajpur.[1] Rachel started in fifth grade at Woodstock in 1977 and graduated from there in 1984. She did well in her studies and was accepted with full scholarship aid by Smith College.

Rachel Rao

But to return to our story! When Rachel returned to India after her accident, she first worked with the Mussoorie Gramin Vikas Samiti (MGVS), which in English means the Mussoorie Village Development Committee. This is the action arm of the Rajpur Christian Retreat and Study Center.

MGVS was working in villages in the hills above Rajpur when Rachel arrived and had just added a community health component to its program. Women, already organized and active, looked to Rachel for help in training village health workers and in the formation of a Mahilla Mandal, an association of village women. One high point of her experience was accompanying a group of eighteen of these women on a field trip to a Sarvodaya (Gandhian) Ashram sixty miles back in the hills behind Mussoorie. There, she and the Chamasari village women who were with her met a large number of other hill women, members of the Mahilla Mandals organized by the ashram. The women they met had been active in forest conservation projects and in combating alcoholism and the use of alcohol. The Chamsari women returned full of enthusiasm, singing songs and shouting slogans they had learned from their new friends.

When Rachel returned to Smith College the next summer, she was convinced she wanted to become a doctor and return to India to work in community health. Unfortunately, due to the lack of financial resources and an undergraduate degree that would qualify her for medical school in India, she was not able to pursue her plans. Instead, she went on to a master's degree program in public health at the University of California in Los Angeles.

The Presbyterian Church (U.S.A.) paid for Rachel's return to India at the end of her first year at UCLA to do field research on family planning practices and attitudes among women she had gotten to know while working with MGVS. The following year, after completing her degree, Rachel was invited to take charge of the MGVS program as coordinator, a position she held for the next three years. This time, the PC(USA) provided a grant to cover her salary and other expenses during the time she was in India.

During the three years that Rachel served as coordinator, MGVS became more and more involved in women's issues and women's rights. Working with other hill-area non-governmental organizations, Rachel and her MGVS team ran a series of training workshops related to the new Panchayti Raj Bill passed by Parliament. For the first time, village people were to participate in the election of leaders at all levels of local self-government (village, block, and district) with a mandate that at least one-third of those elected had to be women. Through these workshops women learned about their new voting rights, voting procedures, how to run for office, and how to participate actively and responsibly as Panchayat members if elected. Inspired by this experience, Rachel decided to go on to law school when she left MGVS in 1997. After giving attention to the social and civil rights of women, Rachel is now concentrating on the legal rights of women.

Robert Alter is a former mission worker in India.

NOTE

1. Though formally an interdenominational mission school for children of North American missionaries, Woodstock is now an autonomous Christian international school with a strong sense of purpose and mission. Presbyterian missionaries still serve at Woodstock, and the school continues to provide a first-class education to the children of missionaries and Christian workers, now mostly Indians and other Asians. Rachel is a prime example of the kind of training in leadership that the school provides to these children. She has said repeatedly that she wouldn't be where she is if it weren't for Woodstock. —Editor

Teruko Ohashi Sugimoto: Breaking New Ground in Medical Social Work

by Margaret Flory

Fifty years ago I spent the summer of 1948 teaching at the Tokyo Women's Christian College under the sponsorship of the Presbyterian Church (U.S.A.). Japan was the first stop on a mission among the students of Asia that took me to three of Japan's enemy countries, Korea, the Philippines, and China. On the night before my departure from Tokyo, the YWCA students held a farewell service around the lily pond. With candles lighting up their faces, their gifts were presented, one of which was a beautiful lantern-lamp with the engraving on the wooden box: "Because you have helped us to walk in the light." There was also a tiny Japanese doll with the flags in its arms of the former enemy countries surrounding the flag of Japan and a brocaded booklet with pictures and messages from six senior students. The book was addressed to "All the Students in the World Who Are Our Friends in Christ." Each student had written a plea for forgiveness and for friendship.

As I read the messages the next day on the flight to Korea, I realized the qualities of faith and commitment in their lives and I wondered what the future had in store for them. I wondered especially about the destiny of Teruko Ohashi, whose balance of beauty, intelligence, and winsomeness was so impressive. She had written:

> I believe that there is no barrier between nations when we meet through Christianity, and it is in this way that peace in the world will come. Our friendship in a small way is bringing real peace to the world. Although we are far away from each other, our prayers are always with yours and we are one in Christ. Let us become stronger in our efforts of doing his will and working for a perfect peace of the world.

At that moment in that plane I could not have anticipated the amazing impact of the book and the doll and the way these simple pleas for reconciliation would mute enmities and produce ties of friendship among the youth of Asian nations and our own. Nor could I have realized how fully these students would be a part of my destiny for the next fifty years.

A transforming event in Teruko Ohashi's life came later that same year when she was baptized in the Seijo Protestant Church, the only Christian in her family. About that time she began corresponding with the members of the student Christian fellowship in Beaver College near Philadelphia, who had entrusted me with a very poignant letter of reconciliation addressed to Japanese students. In her response, she expressed her own personal longing for reconciliation. By the time of her arrival in the United States in 1952 to begin her study at Beaver College, I had become director of a new Office of Student World Relations with the responsibility of the scholarship program for foreign students (later to be known as Leadership Development) and was serving as the Presbyterian Church's advisor to all Presbyterian-related international students. The office became a home base in the United States for what we called the World Family Circle. When Teruko graduated from Beaver College in 1954 with a major in sociology and social work, she received the William Sargent Award given annually to an outstanding member of the graduating class. During this time at Beaver College she worked for a year at the University of Pennsylvania Hospital as part of her field work assignment.

Teruko Ohashi Sugimoto

In September 1954, she entered the School of Social Work at the University of Michigan on the prestigious Barbour scholarship designated for the education of women leaders from Asia. Two years later she graduated with a master's degree in social work and with membership in the Phi Kappa Phi Honor Society. Teruko recently summarized the meaningful directions for life absorbed during her years of study in the United States. She gives the Presbyterian Church credit for steering her into a helping profession and directing her toward caring Christian concern in her approach to life and work. She spoke at many churches, church camps, and conferences, stressing always the meaning of Christian reconciliation. "Such abundant personal exchange and communication," she writes, "formed lifelong friendships."

Because of her personal and leadership qualities, it was natural that she should be invited by Presbyterian Women in 1956 to join the East Asia Women's Reconciliation Team. How well I remember Margaret Shannon, team leader, describing the scene of Teruko meeting her parents in the Tokyo International Airport after a separation of four years. Teruko bowed, then moved slowly and serenely toward them, stopping to bow as they moved toward each other. There was no hugging or crying out—just one last deep bow as they stood face to face. For the outsiders it was a remarkable introduction to Japanese culture. Teruko traveled with the team throughout Japan, sharing the experience of her U. S. years of study.

Teruko's first employment after returning to Japan was as a caseworker at Yodogawa Christian Hospital in Osaka City in cooperation with a Presbyterian missionary, June Lamb. The Department of Social Work was established with Teruko as the first Japanese medical social worker in Japan. Margaret Shannon always spoke of life unfolding and so it has for Teruko in a very special way. In 1959 she married Masamitsu Sugimoto, a Christian doctor, and accompanied him to the United States for three years of training. During these years Teruko pursued her career through employment as social work supervisor at the University of Minnesota Hospital and Henry Ford Hospital. She also served as lecturer at the School of Social Work at Wayne University in Detroit.

That she has been eminently successful in the launching and development of medical social work as a career is attested by the record. Even as she was involved in teaching and casework she completed her work for a PhD in sociology from Kwansei Gakuin University and published her first book in 1966 entitled *Case Work in the Medical Field*. A pioneering effort, it was the first textbook published in Japan in the field of medical social work. She has written and lectured widely in addition to her regular teaching at Kwansei Gakuin University and Hyogo College of Medicine. She is still lecturing at Kwansei University and is now professor emerita at the Hyogo College of Medicine. Dr. Sugimoto belongs to eight academic societies relating to social work and social welfare, serving on the boards of trustees of several.

In addressing medical students and social work majors, Teruko frequently concentrates on the values derived from Christianity as well as values from

Asian thought in Confucianism and Buddhism. Here in her own words is a description of family relationships:

> As a very studious Christian, my husband has helped me in preparing content for teaching with precise Bible quotations, which I always use in my speeches and lectures wherever they are given. . . . I have been able to help develop expert leaders of the next generation in the field of social work in health and medicine in Japan. However, above all, I was taught and given so much from those who needed my help, and through relationships with young students, co-workers and my family.

Though members of her family attend different churches, both Protestant and Catholic, Teruko reminded me that "we feel one in Christ as a family. . . . We are all in helping professions to which you, Margaret, introduced me in the United States back in 1952. . . . You . . . have helped me . . . to walk the path intended by God for me to walk. I will certainly continue to walk the same path, until God tells me to stop."[1]

Recently, through the Year with Education, I again met June Lamb, Teruko's close colleague at the mission hospital in Osaka. We shared the sense of her personhood, the uniqueness of her vision, and the unusual quality of her Christian leadership in a new profession. June describes her with these words, "serene, sincere, and effective," while I choose to quote Lord Byron:

> She walks in beauty, like the night
> Of cloudless climes and starry skies,
> And all that's best of dark and bright
> Meet in her aspect and her eyes . . .[2]

Margaret Flory, a visionary, instigator, and major supporter of the International Leadership Development Program, was director of the Office of Student Relations for the UPC(USA). (Her article entitled "Walking in One Company" in Church and Society, *November/December 1986–January/February 1987, serves as a brief, but fascinating history of the International Leadership Development Program to that date.)*

NOTES

1. Fax from Teruko Sugimoto to Margaret Flory, July 1998.
2. George Noel Gordon, Lord Byron, "She Walks in Beauty," in Byron: Poems (New York: Alfred A. Knopf, 1994).

Elsa Tamez: Passion for the Excluded Ones

by Ross Kinsler

I was born in Monterrey, Mexico, in a poor neighborhood that was said to be dangerous. I grew up together with four brothers and four sisters, my father and mother, and an aunt who never married. She was also like a mother.

The house was very small: a living room, a bedroom, a kitchen, plus a back yard. I think that is the reason I grew up in the street, playing happily in the mud. (At that time, the streets were not paved.) When night fell, my mother would call and we would go in to sleep. The floor of the living room and the bedroom would be covered with our bodies.

My mother worked the whole day. She was the first to get up and the last to go to bed. I remember that she always prayed a lot. Kneeling, hidden, I don't know what things she would pray to God about. My father, who was almost never at home, could do anything, sell anything, and eat anything. He sold lottery tickets, oranges, mangos, smuggled goods from the United States, chickens, eggs, avocados. . . . My older brothers and sisters were very embarrassed when they had to go out to sell "house-to-house." I didn't have to do it because I was one of the youngest. We bought everything on credit: furniture, watches, even food. We were always being visited by the creditors. We had to make up a thousand lies when we didn't have the money to pay them.

I hardly ever drink milk. Sometimes I think that is because, when I was a little girl, my mother would give me milk hidden from my brothers and sisters so that they wouldn't ask for some, too. My mother gave me milk because I was very thin and she was afraid that I would get tuberculosis.

My mother always encouraged us to study. She thought that if we studied hard we could get out of poverty. She had been a teacher in the countryside, so she could help us with our homework when we needed it. At that time, when we would leave our neighborhood to go downtown or to another neighborhood, we were ashamed to say where we lived. It was degrading to us, so we would say that we lived in the next neighborhood, one that was a bit better than ours. My mother instilled in us a great sense of dignity, but it was very difficult to maintain this sense in an industrial society as stratified as Monterrey.

With these words, Dr. Elsa Tamez began her address at the 1997 Kirchentag celebration in Germany. They reveal the roots and the identity of the person who today is known around the world as one of the great biblical scholars, theologians, and ecumenical figures of our time. Running through all her work is a passion for little girls and boys and men and women who are threatened not only by poverty, but by all the machinations of modernity, urbanization, economic exclusion, and social marginalization.

In the 1970s and 1980s, Elsa's message was very much in tune with "the option for the poor" so prominent in Latin American liberation theology. She was one of the first Latin Americans to begin to hold what might be called "the option for women." And she has joined wholeheartedly in solidarity with Latin America's indigenous peoples in their struggles for liberation and full participation in church and society. In 1997 she spoke of "the many faces of poverty" at a consultation of the Ecumenical Association of Third World Theologians, and she currently chairs that body's work on women's concerns.

Elsa Tamez

This passion for the "excluded one" shines through every presentation that Elsa is called on to make. In recent years she has given major addresses and lectureships in many parts of Latin America, North America, Europe, Africa, and Asia. She is in much demand among Protestant and Roman Catholics audiences. She shared the keynote address of the World Alliance of Reformed Churches Assembly in Hungary in 1997. But she is careful to limit her travels in order to attend to her own family, which includes a husband and two teenagers, and her teaching and research and writing in Costa Rica.

The best memories of my childhood come from the Presbyterian church in my neighborhood. I remember the trips, the activities with children and young people, Bible school, the contests, and the triumphs that I had in those contests. I believe that was the best social circle for the boys and girls of that neighborhood because we felt so accepted. I realize now that it was very conservative in its theology. . . .

When I was eighteen, I went to Costa Rica to study theology at the Latin American Biblical Seminary. With the passing of time, my experience of God changed radically. Even though I have always had a very special relationship with God, upon studying theology, my spirituality became revolutionary and ecumenical. The Central American situation demanded that God be thought of in terms of commitment and solidarity. The disappeared, the tortured, the innocent people imprisoned, the massacres of indigenous peoples demanded the practice of justice as an integral part of Christian faith. For those of us inside the church, this was the structural sin that had to be combated in our work for justice. God, in solidarity with the poor, was our guide. Jesus Christ showed us the way of justice, a difficult road that sometimes meant giving one's life for brothers and sisters. We felt the necessity of transforming unjust structures for a new society.

Elsa specialized first in Old Testament studies, and she wrote her first thesis on "The Bible of the Oppressed," an investigation of the Old Testament language for poverty and oppression. The small book that came out of that research has been published in many languages. She also studied for a graduate degree in literature and linguistics at the National University. Her unpublished thesis there was on the Song of Solomon. She joined the faculty at the Latin American Biblical Seminary in 1979, continuing in the field of Old Testament. In 1986 she went with her family to Lausanne, Switzerland, and undertook doctoral studies in New Testament and theology. Continuing her concern for justice, she wrote her dissertations there on "Justification by Faith from a Latin American Perspective." It has been published by Abingdon Press under the title *The Amnesty of Grace*.

For many years Elsa has carried out many responsibilities at the Ecumenical Department of Research (DEI), which is also located in San Jose and which is dedicated to training "base community" leaders and promoting dialogue among leading Latin American theologians. She continues to participate in DEI workshops, consultations, and publications. She is also one of the team of Latin American biblical scholars who publish a Latin American journal of biblical interpretation, RIBLA, in Spanish and Portuguese, and who run a yearly six-month training program for budding Bible teachers and scholars in the region. In addition Elsa has for many years guided the work of ecumenical theological education for the World Council of Churches.

In 1995 Elsa was elected president of the Latin American Biblical Seminary. She immediately initiated a campaign to build a new campus on a piece of unused property of the seminary, utilizing current downtown buildings as a source for ongoing income. The campaign is called One Million Women, and it incarnates her vision of enabling people all over the world, rich and poor alike, to participate by making one-dollar contributions with the names of women they would like to have remembered. At the time of this writing, names have been gathered from 116 countries, and the main building of the new campus is almost completed.

In 1997, after an intensive process, the seminary was recognized as the Latin American Biblical University by the National Council for Private University Higher Education. This represents no real change in the seminary's orientation or programming, but it does mean that its degrees will now have official recognition, opening doors for service and witness and further study by its graduates. Elsa has insisted on strengthening the seminary's middle school program of theological studies as well, which directly or indirectly serves a much wider constituency of local church leaders who will never attain university-level studies.

Elsa Tamez is not yet fifty years old, but even if she lives to be 100 she will never lose that special sensitivity that not only speaks for but draws out the humanity and dignity of all who have the opportunity to hear her, to read her many books, to participate in workshops and consultation with her, or best of all, to work closely with her on a daily basis.

Dr. Ross Kinsler is a mission worker in Costa Rica, member
of the Interim Collegial Directorate of the Latin American Biblical
University, and close colleague of Elsa Tamez.

[Editor's Note: The Latin American Biblical University recently celebrated their seventy-fifth anniversary under the theme "The Biblical Jubilee: Time to Recreate Life."]

Amnuay Tapingkae: Born to Serve

by Martha Butt

In the late 1940s a Buddhist family in rural, northern Thailand decided to send their son to The Prince Royal's College, a Christian elementary and high school twenty-five kilometers away in Chiang Mai. Before setting off for school, the father told his boy, "Son, we're sending you to this school to get a good education, but not Christianity." The young Amnuay Tapingkae did well in school and attended chapel daily.

When Amnuay was thirteen, he became very ill with typhoid fever and was admitted to the nearby McCormick Hospital, the Presbyterian mission hospital, which was known for outstanding care. The boy remembers lying in bed, nearly delirious with fever, and hearing the doctor tell his parents that he was sorry they had no medicine to make their son better. After hearing this news, the boy then overheard his parents say that they feared they were going to lose their only son and that they must, therefore, find a new son to adopt.

To his parent's delight, the boy did not die. After several months he was able to return to school. Because of his experience in the hospital, however, he became more interested in Christian teachings. He listened carefully to the message of God's steadfastness. He thought to himself, "God would never give up on me as my parents were about to do." Before graduating from high school, the boy decided to become a Christian. At first his parents were very upset, but in time they respected his decision and new religious faith, although they themselves remained Buddhist.

Going on to devote his life to education for which he received numerous advanced degrees and honors, Amnuay Tapingkae completed his distinguished service as president of Payap University, the first Protestant and first private university in Thailand. But that's getting ahead of the story!

Given a scholarship to attend Illinois College in the mid-1950s, Amnuay found an atmosphere of friendship and fellowship that greatly influenced his ideas about education and service. Both in and out of the classroom, Amnuay was involved with professors, classmates, and community people. He was especially influenced by President Caine, a community and church leader who was smiling, calm, and accessible to the students, serving as model for the style of college president that Amnuay would later become.

At the same time Amnuay was active in the First Presbyterian Church, where he was elected deacon and chairman of the Christian Student Fellowship and where he experienced the importance of linking service and faith. He also worked as a busboy at the Elm City Cafe. From these experiences he learned that education is a holistic experience in which life and education go hand in hand.

During times of uncertainty in these years, Amnuay trusted in God's guidance. He tells of the summer he traveled throughout the United States volunteering as a youth leader at church camps. This experience helped him formulate the theological and spiritual understanding of his ministry. After completing an assignment in Happy Valley, Maryland, a camp leader took him out for a farewell dinner of clam chowder, a favorite dish. While they were eating, she asked not once, but twice, "Tap (as they called him at the camp), where will you go now?" And twice Amnuay replied, "Wherever the Greyhound bus takes me. God will lead me. He never lets me down." Finally the camp leader said, "I am going to my home in Maryland. I have no sons. Will you come with me and be my 'Thainese' son?" Amnuay said there is no such thing as "Thainese," but, yes, he would love to go. Once again his prayers had been answered.

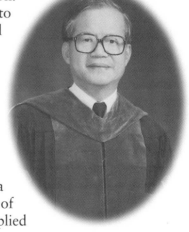

At the time of graduation from Illinois College in 1959, President Caine called Amnuay into his office to tell him some good news. Amnuay had been given a Presidential Fellowship to the University of Chicago for graduate study. Amnuay replied honestly, "Thank you for the honor, Mr. President, but I want to go home. I am homesick." The wise president did not

Amnuay Tapingkae

insist that Amnuay stay on and provided an airplane ticket for him to return to Thailand.

Upon return to Thailand, Amnuay told God he was ready for any assignment. In his calling as lecturer, and then dean of the Faculty of Education at

Chiang Mai University, he represented a Christian presence at this secular, government institution during its early years of existence. At that time, Amnuay undertook his first effort in Christian leadership development when he helped to establish the Crystal Spring House, a student center for Christian and non-Christian students at the university.

The first big challenge of his career came when the president and most leaders of the university were away. Five thousand students staged a protest. The three university deans who were present were called upon to solve the problem. Of these Amnuay was the youngest and the only Christian. The first two spoke to the students, but few listened. Amnuay prayed to God to help him convince students that the problem could be solved peacefully. He then got up and told the students three things: "First, I am your friend and want to solve the problem with you; second, if you trust me, I will negotiate with the government, but first you must disperse; and third, if I fail to resolve the problem, I will resign from my position as dean." The students accepted his proposal and dispersed. Amnuay negotiated an acceptable solution with the government. Later when he asked the students why they trusted him, they said it was because he was willing to lose his job and position for their sake. Amnuay knew that as a Christian servant he did not need to hang on to his position. God would always take care of him.

Another hard decision came later when Amnuay was asked to accept the presidency of Payap University. At the time he had a very important post representing the Royal Thai Government to an intergovernment organization based in Singapore. He was on his way to becoming one of the highest ranking civil servants in Thailand. He prayed about the request to come back to Chiang Mai and lead the Christian University. Twice he declined the invitation and suggested other leaders for the post, but the search committee came back to him a third time and insisted they wanted Amnuay. So he accepted God's call.

When Amnuay first arrived at Payap University, the new campus was little more than a swampland. Along with a team of dedicated colleagues, he built a comprehensive Christian university. Amnuay's initial challenges included convincing the already existing nursing and theology school alumni to join Payap. Guided by faith and prayer, he led the staff and raised the necessary funds to establish a truly comprehensive Christian university.

Early on in his Payap presidency, he faced a big challenge from the faculty association, led that year by a Buddhist instructor. They confronted Amnuay with the fact that there was a cross in the chapel at this Thai university where

Buddhism is the national religion and demanded that a statue of Buddha be placed on campus. The Buddhist teachers believed they had a constitutional right to do this and said if the president refused they would go to the highest authorities. After prayer Amnuay went to meet with the faculty committee and explained that Payap University was one of a few Christian institutions in Thailand, that the university's leadership was concerned about the spiritual and moral fiber of students, that the King of Thailand's desire to have responsible and useful citizens was appreciated and taken very seriously, and that the Christian leadership wanted to teach honesty and responsibility in order to help the country develop. Then he asked the faculty leaders to allow Payap University to perform its task faithfully with both Christian and non-Christian staff working together. As a Christian, Amnuay told them he could not honor their request to have a Buddha image erected on campus and, further, that he was willing to die for his faith. Then he asked the faculty representatives if they were willing to die for theirs. The issue was never raised again and the subject was put to rest forever.

Dr. Amnuay Tapingkae served Payap University as president for nearly twenty years. He led the institution as it grew from 200 students to more than 6,000. Today, in "retirement," Dr. Amnuay Tapingkae works as hard as ever to serve his church and country. The accomplishments of this man over the years have been many. Surely his early training in Christian institutions, both in Thailand and abroad, prompted his belief that the teaching of God's love is fundamental to the idea that "the heart of education is the education of the heart."

Martha Butt is a mission worker, serving in the administration of Payap University in Thailand.

"I appreciate very much the assistance I have gotten from the International Leadership Development Program. This program gives to many people the opportunity to receive an education which allows them to face the challenges of social justice and spiritual and political liberation that their societies need."

Elisée Musemakweli of Rwanda

K. H. Ting (Ding Guangxun):
A Unique Interpreter of the Christian Faith

by Janice Wickeri

K. H. Ting (Ding Guangxun) returned to international prominence in church circles in the 1980s as the president of the China Christian Council and chairperson of the Three-Self Patriotic Movement of Protestant Churches in China. (Three-self means self-governing, self-supporting, self-propagating.) It was a time when normal church life was resuming following the Cultural Revolution, and Christianity in China entered a period of rapid growth.

A graduate of St. John's University in Shanghai in 1942, K. H. Ting received his MA degree from Union Theological Seminary in New York in 1948. Later, Bishop Ting would have the unique ability to interpret the regeneration of Christianity in China to the worldwide church because of his very concrete experience of church life in the West, not as a student, but in positions dealing with students and mission issues.

In the late 1940s, he was received by a forward-looking Canadian Student Christian Movement to educate students about the role of Christian churches in the world. He traveled throughout Canada, speaking in universities and writing articles for the Student Christian Movement newsletter, *The Canadian Student*. He also traveled throughout the United States and in South America.

Lois Wilson, a past president of the World Council of Churches, met K. H. Ting during his time in Canada. She says, "He helped us to understand the tangled web of motives in the mission practices of the day, as well as the ways the American churches, in this instance, were in captivity to the prevailing understanding of their government as to the demonic nature of communism." Shortly afterwards, in 1951, all foreign missionaries were expelled from China as "cultural imperialists," and Chinese churches withdrew from the World Council of Churches. In the midst of this turmoil, K. H. intentionally returned to China, against the advice of many of his friends overseas. There he served as general secretary of the Christian Literature Society before becoming principal of Nanjing Union Theological Seminary in 1952. In 1955, he was made Bishop of Chekiang (Zhejiang).

Conversant as he was with Western culture and theology, he never forgot that he was Chinese. It has been because of this intentional grounding in his own people and culture that he has functioned so well as a patient advocate and interpreter to the worldwide church of the three-self principle (self-governing, self-supporting, self-propagating) and cooperation with socialism adopted by the church in China. He has shown Christians at home and overseas how religious believers can work together with non-believers for the wider good.

After the Cultural Revolution, Bishop Ting reemerged as a Christian leader and educator in China and as a significant voice for religious interests on a national level. K. H. Ting has been the leader of the church in China needed in the 1980s and 1990s. In spite of difficulties and setbacks, Christianity in China has a higher profile than at any time in its history there. In 1978, Bishop Ting was made a member of the Standing Committee of the Chinese People's Political Consultative Conference and the following year was named a delegate to the National People's Congress. The standing

K. H. Ting

and access this gives him to advocate religious interests at the highest levels has not been well understood overseas, but should not be underestimated. A young (non-Christian) colleague from the United Front Work Department in Beijing has commented that he takes "every opportunity to speak to government officials, especially at national meetings. He would always stand up to criticize transgressions against the rights of religious believers and to protect their rights as citizens to believe." In this role he has been able to interpret government policy and the true character of religion to cadres and government officials at many levels and has been especially active in opposing the idea that religion, in all societies and eras, is "the opiate of the people."

At the same time he has interpreted government religious policy to Christians, especially in terms of the demands of patriotism and the need for registration of churches and meeting points in an effort to ensure all Christian gatherings a legal status. This can be a difficult position and it is one that has at times drawn criticism both at home and overseas. By his own understanding, these are part of Bishop Ting's efforts to both enlarge and maintain the space for religious belief and activity in Chinese society.

As a theological educator, Bishop Ting has introduced students at Nanjing Union Theological Seminary to international theological trends through his courses and lectures, introducing major thinkers and movements and calling for reflection on their relevance to the Chinese situation. He has also sought to broaden students' experience of their heritage as Christians across cultures and borders, quoting church fathers, Western writers, and poets as well as Chinese figures in his sermons and lectures. Advocacy of a democratic style within the church and the rejuvenation of clergy and leadership through the ordination and promotion of younger people have marked Bishop Ting's leadership in the church. His retirement from both national church leadership positions in early 1997 showed his personal commitment to these goals.

Although K. H. Ting is one of the most farsighted theologians in China and is well aware of international theological trends, he has chosen to express his theological insights in a concrete way, speaking both to and from the church. This orientation has been a hallmark of both his theology and his leadership. One of his abiding concerns has been both to make Chinese Christians aware of their membership in the worldwide body of Christ and to demonstrate to generally more conservative Chinese Christians a more tolerant approach to nonbelievers. The encompassing love of which all creation partakes has been a focus of his emphasis on the cosmic Christ and on God as the great lover. He has sought to convey his insight that nothing, including socialist China and the majority of nonbelievers there, lies outside this love of God.

In his remarks during a return visit to New York's Union Seminary in 1994, Bishop Ting quoted Paul in words that could serve as a summary of his experience as well as that of the Chinese church over the last forty years: "'A wide door for effective work has opened to me, and there are many adversaries' (1 Cor. 16:9). It is interesting that the conjunction used is 'and,' not 'but.' This conveys the idea that, in our small way, we are doing an experiment on behalf of the church worldwide."

Janice Wickeri was formerly managing editor of the Research Centre for Translation of the Chinese University of Hong Kong, and is currently editor of the Chinese Theological Review, *published by the Foundation for Theological Education in Southeast Asia.*

John Titaley: A Voice for Dialogue and Social Responsibility

by Jean S. Stoner

ohn Titaley is a man who has become uniquely prepared to respond to the urgent needs of both his Christian community and his nation. Look at the setting of Indonesia in 1998: the fourth most populous country of the world, comprised of 17,000 islands with a large Muslim majority, emerges from a long period of dictatorship into an uncertain political situation fueled by economic instability. One of the currents much in evidence advocates increased "Islamization" of the nation. In these circumstances that foster persecution of minorities and repression of all sorts, how can the Christian community provide a strong positive influence? Only by means of leadership that has been prepared and is ready for the challenges. In this instance we are fortunate that a PC(USA) Leadership Development Scholar has laid the foundation for dealing with these difficult circumstances.

How did this happen? John Titaley was born to a Chinese mother in a Christian family in East Indonesia. Because he was from a "mixed" family, his father did not inherit the land that would normally have been his, so the children needed to get education to prepare for their own futures. After completing his high school studies, John studied theology at Satya Wacana Christian University, where he met a wonderful Muslim woman, Ida, who was studying biology. Ida became Christian and two years later they married.

On completion of his university studies, John was invited to become a lecturer in theology at Satya Wacana. In addition he was ordained as a minister in the Church of West Indonesia and assisted in both a local church and presbytery.

This normal, successful career was good, but both John and the church leaders recognized his potential for a great deal more. In 1986 he was admitted to San Francisco Theological Seminary as a special student and then as a doctoral student in the Graduate Theological Union (GTU) in Inter-Areas studies. Here, working in a rich interdisciplinary and interdenominational setting in the field of Old Testament, he acquired the background that he would soon find to be invaluable in providing critical insights for understanding and working with Muslim brothers and sisters.

In January 1991 when he returned to Indonesia, John Titaley was asked to prepare a graduate program in religion and society for Satya Wacana Christian University in Salatiga. Just eight months later, in the fall of 1991, the graduate program in religion and society started. John was appointed dean of the program, and since 1995 has been dean of an expanded graduate program that includes the field of development studies as well. This expanded program has most ambitious goals. Within a broad goal to enhance the educational level of clergy in Indonesia, the university adopted the more specific objective to prepare its graduates to lead their church members to understand the theological basis for participation in the social and political arena. The goal is to empower Christians to witness among their neighbors and to be able to dialogue with all, Muslims as well as fellow Christians. God's hand is surely visible in the timely development of this program that now stands ready to assist at a critical time.

John Titaley

Dr. Titaley has been a member of the Indonesian Association of Theological Schools since 1991 and chairperson since 1995. From this position he proposed and led the development of a network of all graduate programs in theology in Indonesia. Since 1997 this consortium has been actively supporting enhancement of the education level for ministers in Indonesia from the current requirement of a bachelor's degree.

In addition to his work at the university, Dr. Titaley is also treasurer of the Coordinating Body of Christian Education in Indonesia and the Association for Theological Education in Southeast Asia. He has participated in the accreditation process for theological institutions in other countries in the region on behalf of the association.

Recognition of his outstanding scholarship was accorded when John was invited to participate in the India program of the 1998 Cook Theological Travel Seminar, "Preparing for Witness in Context." In this capacity he presented a paper and was part of a group of six theological professors hosted by Indian theological institutions.

Dr. Titaley is grateful for the opportunity he had as a Leadership Development Scholar. He credits this training and study with equipping him to help strategically prepare the churches of Indonesia to work together with all their compatriots to strive for a better future for the nation. His graduate study gave John the breadth of vision and the leadership skills required for these special tasks. As he looks to the future, John, speaking of himself and his wife, Ida, said, "It has been our prayer that God is willing to use our lives for God's work." We trust that God will continue to prepare John to meet future challenges and that he and his family will continue to be blessed.

Jean S. Stoner is former Interim Coordinator for the Office of Global Education and International Leadership Development in the Worldwide Ministries Division, PC(USA), and Coordinator of the 1998 Cook Theological Travel Seminar.

José Luis Velazco: Churchman and Prophet, a Rare Combination

by Salatiel Palomino

At the age of twelve or thirteen years, José Luis Velazco experienced an inclination toward the Christian ministry in his native Zitacuaro, a small city in the State of Michoacán. After completing his high school (at what today we know as Presbyterian Pan American School in Kingsville, Texas) and some college education in North Carolina, he returned to Mexico to take care of his ailing mother. Encouraged by his friend, the Rev. Ariel Gomez, he studied at the Presbyterian Theological Seminary in Mexico from 1948 to 1951. He was ordained to the ministry of Word and Sacrament by the Presbytery of the South in Morelia, Michoacán, in 1953. Since that time he has served pastorates in several rural and urban churches, while engaging in some formal studies at the University of Washington in Seattle and the Ecumenical Institute of Bossey, Switzerland, under the sponsorship of the International Leadership Development Program.

This theological training enabled him to carry out a distinguished and varied ministry: as stated clerk of the General Assembly of the National Presbyterian Church of Mexico (1962, 1966–1968); as secretary of Christian Education for the same denomination (1959–1962); as director of the Ecumenical Youth Program of the former United Presbyterian Church in the U.S.A.; as director of the Student Program of the Presbyterian Church of Mexico (1965–1970); and as pastor of the Hispanic Church in Washington, D.C., for three years. He also worked for the Ethnic Minority Affairs Program of the former Presbyterian Church in the United States in Atlanta, and was director and editor of the Casa Unida de Publicaciones, a Protestant publishing house in Mexico, from 1979 through 1990. Through the years he has taught at both the Presbyterian and the Methodist seminaries in Mexico City. Married to Cherie White, a Methodist missionary, he is the father of four children: José, eighteen, Luis, seventeen, Iliana, twelve, and Byron, eight. Cherie currently teaches Old Testament and church history at the Methodist Seminary and serves as dean.

The Presbyterian Church in Mexico has been blessed by God through the inspiring life, the many gifts, and the multifaceted ministry of the Rev. José Luis Velazco. He has certainly been one of the most influential servants of God in this portion of Christ's body. His rich personality, the solidity and firmness of his faith in and commitment to Christ, the wisdom and scholarship found in his numerous contributions both in writing and in public speech, and his able and progressive leadership have made a significant difference in the building up of the church in Mexico.

Perhaps what has most characterized the Rev. Velazco's leadership style is—in the best Ephesian (4:11) tradition—the balance between the pastoral and the educational elements of sound Christian ministry. He has combined them in a rich, productive, and delicate way. His modeling of this biblical insight into ministry has had a permanent influence on his parishioners, his colleagues, and his many seminary students and disciples over the years.

José Luis Velazco

My first recollection of his ministry goes back to the years when, as a young member of my local church, I had the opportunity to enjoy his leading a special workshop on stewardship. What impressed me most, however, was his masterful teaching of new hymns on Christian stewardship. The way he explained the lyrics and the theology of the hymns, the way he played the piano with artistic precision, the tone of his well-educated voice in singing, all of this, was conducive to a delightful experience of worship, of learning and spiritual edification that characterized not only that particular workshop, but the whole of his ministry.

Another story reminds me of the profound theological contribution of José Luis Velazco. The whole senior class at the Presbyterian Seminary in Mexico once had a little quarrel with the faculty that had "insulted" them, proud "theologians," by scheduling a Christian education course for the last semester. In those days, prejudiced and inexperienced pastors-to-be held Christian education in very low regard. The course, however, was taught by José Luis

Velazco, and it turned out to be, according to the unanimous consensus of the class, the best theological experience they had during the four years of their seminary education. It was a course full of pleasant but solid learning activities, thought-provoking discussion, insightful and practical knowledge, modern creative educational and theological thinking. That has been the result and the character of all the activities and ministries Brother Velazco has carried out in the Mexican church, whether they were conferences on faith and culture, stewardship workshops, Sunday school institutes, ecumenical seminars, theological encounters, long-term pastorates, formal seminary courses, or brief sermons and addresses.

In an age in search of expedient effectiveness and shallow practicalities, of shrewd political maneuvering and thirst for power in both state and church, men and women of principle and vision are very rare. In this sense, the life and gifts of José Luis Velazco have been a blessing and an asset for the church of Christ in Mexico. His leadership and influence have incorporated precisely these virtues. The Rev. Velazco has served the church with love and loyalty, providing it with able leadership, sound educational practices, and spiritual vision. He has been a man whose life has been devoted to the Lord for service in the church and on behalf of the weakest members of society.

"Along with our ministry to others, we have been blessed by the love and ministry of others toward us. . . . All along we have found how important and useful the training and resources we obtained through the Presbyterian Church (U.S.A.) have been. Our training program has provided vision, strength, and orientation for a solid and, hopefully, fruitful ministry geared toward the formation of new generations of faithful and creative servants of God."

Dr. Salatiel Palomino, pastor and professor of theology, and PC(USA) International Leadership Development Scholar

At the same time, as a churchman, he has never been a servant of institutional interests; rather, he has acted as a promoter of justice, an advocate for truth and real Christian obedience and love. In doing this, he has taken a firm stance against injustice and mere expediency in ecclesiastical and social matters. He has defended Christian principles with conviction and integrity, a prophetic stance that has gained him not a few enemies. His public defense of the gospel and of his convictions, however, has been done with lucidity, grace, generosity, and a gentleman's respect for his adversaries. Indeed, his brilliant insight into many debatable issues and his mastery of logical argument and theological depth have gained him many friends.

In all respects, the people of God in Mexico have been guided, edified, and blessed by the life and influence of this powerful but gentle, nonintimidating, friendly prophet—and my dear mentor and friend. And in spite of his retirement status, José Luis Velazco is still learning, still teaching. He will earn a master's degree at Columbia Theological Seminary in Decatur in May 1999. His thesis on "The Significance of Dietrich Bonhoeffer for Protestant Christians and Churches in Mexico" has already been accepted. And he continues teaching at the Methodist seminary in Mexico City. Prophet, teacher, churchman, and theologian to the end!

Dr. Salatiel Palomino is a pastor and professor of theology, Mexico City.

[Editor's Note: Dr. Palomino is also one of the outstanding International Leadership Development Scholars. He most recently served as dean of the Faculty and Professor of Theology at the Presbyterian Theological Seminary in Mexico City. Dr. Palomino received his doctorate at Princeton University, assisted by the International Leadership Development Program of the PC(USA).]

Jean-Samuel Zoe and Rose Zoe-Obianga: They Speak with Authority and Uncommon Wisdom

by Guy Bekaert

JEAN-SAMUEL ZOE

I remember very well my first encounter with Jean-Samuel Zoe. It was in October 1960 at the beginning of the school year at the University of Strasbourg in France, where I was in the third year of theology. Jean-Samuel had just arrived from Cameroon and I certainly didn't know then that it would be the beginning of a wonderful friendship. Jean-Samuel Zoe was born in Ebolawa in South Cameroon in 1937 where one could find a large hospital, schools, and a church that has been for many years the largest Presbyterian congregation in the world. Jean-Samuel came from a strong Christian family. His father was a catechist. People still talk about his zeal and ardor in preaching the gospel.

Jean-Samuel Zoe

But let's go back to this year 1960 when a young Cameroonian man was entering a new world. One can imagine his enthusiasm and hope, but also his apprehension, even fear, at being confronted with a very different environment, culturally and geographically. As it turned out, he would be away from home for eleven years to study theology, receiving on the way his STM (master of sacred theology), another degree in the French system in two years, and finally his doctorate.

I left Strasbourg in 1962 and I didn't see Jean-Samuel again until 1975 when my wife and I arrived in Cameroon for our first assignment with the United Presbyterian Church in the U.S.A. We lived about 200 yards apart and so had the chance to meet regularly. They were married with children; the first one was born in 1967.

I quickly discovered that Jean-Samuel had become my master in terms of theological knowledge and wisdom. He was at that time the dean of the Yaounde Faculty of Protestant Theology, while teaching ethics and systematic theology. Students were already coming from all over Africa and some from Europe.

Unfortunately for me both Jean-Samuel and Rose would go in 1977 to New York to study at Union Theological Seminary. Jean-Samuel was a visiting scholar doing research in order to complete his PhD later on in France. Rose also studied at Union in the field of leadership. While in America Jean-Samuel traveled to Costa Rica and several other countries in connection with his research on liberation theology. He became a specialist on this subject and quite well known in Cameroon and other countries in Africa. Though a "specialist," there was no arrogance in

Rose Zoe-Obianga

his knowledge. On the contrary Jean-Samuel was quite reserved with regard to this subject, always respecting the context and careful of too quick an assessment of local settings.

Rose and Jean-Samuel, always our good and faithful friends, went back to Cameroon in 1981. On their return I discovered the blessings that were a result of their training abroad, results that were visible on several levels:

1. In their own church, the Presbyterian Church of Cameroon (EPC). It is certain that their strong and extensive training had given them authority, not only as member or chairpersons of various committees, but also in dialogue with leaders of the church. When they would raise their voices (mezza voce for Jean Samuel, fortissimo for Rose), they would inspire respect. Leaders of synods or presbyteries would seek their advice. Rose has been education secretary for the EPC for years, and as such in charge of hundreds of schools (primary and secondary). She also served as the general secretary for the EPC Women's Association. Their commitment was unquestionable—constant, firm, and faithful—despite the time spent away with speaking engagements and despite unavoidable problems or quarrels within the church.

2. In other churches, Protestant and Roman Catholic. Both Jean-Samuel and Rose were constantly in demand for speaking engagements, conferences, and so forth. They enjoyed this and found it difficult to say "no" to those they could not accept. In addition they participated in countless ecumenical services and prayer meetings.

3. For individuals and communities. Their long residence in France and in the United States and their studies gave Rose and Jean-Samuel a kind of aura, a kind of prestige that made them "chief" in an African way. They were constantly solicited for advice and direction in many areas. Jean-Samuel often had to drive 200 miles on poor roads to go back to his village or other places to serve as an advisor in community discussions and to settle disputes. I personally would never have made an important decision concerning my work, theological issues, or our churches without meeting with Rose and Jean-Samuel for advice. I have an immense respect for them.

ROSE ZOE-OBIANGA

It would take a whole chapter to talk about Rose's work on African and world levels. Yet she remained humble and grateful for the opportunity to serve. She once said, "God has been deeply and powerfully active in everything I am doing!" At the same time she was aware of the confidence that her educational preparation had given her to serve the church at all levels. Let us mention but a few of her achievements and contributions.

Rose served as vice president of the All African Conference of Churches (AACC) from 1992 to 1997, eventually becoming a nominee for the position of AACC president when Desmond Tutu completed his mandate. Rose belonged to and contributed her knowledge and experience in various groups and committees. At the international level, she was a member of the Sub-Unit/Advisory Group on Human Rights of the World Council of Churches (WCC), (1975–1983), the Sub-Unit of the Dialogue with People of Other Faiths, and the Unit on Education, Mission and Health (1984–1990). She was an integral part of the Justice, Peace, Integrity of Creation initiative of the WCC, and worked hard on the WCC Working Group on Women (Unit III).

The Ecumenical Association of Third World Theologians and the Circle of Concerned African Women claimed her talents as well. I had the pleasure of working under her direction in the preparation of the General Assembly of the

World Alliance of Reformed Churches held in Yaounde in 1995.

At one point in my life I questioned the usefulness of spending so much money on education for sometimes an uncertain result. However, after twenty years spent in different countries in Africa, I'm convinced that we have to do even more with this program of International Leadership Development.

While I'm writing these lines I have in front of me the "Mission Meeting Minutes of 1954" held in Abele, where Jean-Samuel was born seventeen years before. It just so happens that I was at that meeting. There were then more than 100 missionaries in the field. Sixty-two attended the meeting. One can find their names in the minutes which state, "Visitors and Guests [followed by the names of four African pastors]. Moved, seconded, and carried that these men be received as corresponding members of mission, with privileges of the floor."

That was almost forty-five years ago! When I see Rose and Jean-Samuel and many others that I have known personally (from Rwanda, Congo, and so forth), I am very glad that the Office of Global Education and International Leadership Development has helped to make the transition that so changed the ratio of missionaries and African leaders.

SOLI DEO GLORIA!

The Rev. Guy Bekaert, a former mission worker in Cameroon, is Western Africa Coordinator of the Project for Evangelism and Church Growth in Africa.

"At one point in my life I questioned the usefulness of spending so much money on education for sometimes an uncertain result. However, after twenty years spent in different countries in Africa, I'm convinced that we have to do even more with this program of International Leadership Development."

Guy Bekaert, former mission co-worker in Cameroon

A Glimpse of the Future

By now you are surely convinced, if there was ever a doubt in your mind, of the incredible payoff our investment in educating church leaders has had. We Presbyterians should be proud that previous generations were such good stewards and invested in people, trusting God to "give the increase." But the story has not ended! The International Leadership Development program continues to fund over 100 international scholars each year. We are currently supporting many new church leaders selected by our partner churches overseas. All of them have had their basic university education. Most study theology and religion in order to train other leaders at home. But some churches have asked for assistance in training persons to meet new challenges of ministry and mission. Here are some examples of our scholars in 1998.

- A Christian farmer from India is studying in Japan for a year at the Asian Rural Institute together with other Asian Christians. They are all looking at sustainable farming techniques and learning good leadership skills so that they can return home and share these new learnings with others.
- Some churches are still using hymnals that U.S. mission personnel brought with them decades ago. Many churches are involved in supporting young musicians who are writing new hymns, with melodies and rhythms from their own culture. We support some musicians who are studying to do just this.
- One of the newer requests for scholarship assistance is coming from Reformed churches in Central Europe. After living in isolation from churches outside the ex-Soviet Union, these churches are entering the twenty-first century with libraries that have had no new books since the early 1950s. Assistance has been requested to send younger leaders outside Central Europe to study abroad for a year in order to bring back fresh thoughts and new

ideas to share with their churches.

- The Rev. Elisee Musemakweli is a young leader from the Presbyterian Church of Rwanda, finishing his doctoral degree at Brussels Protestant Seminary. When the fighting and genocide occurred in Rwanda in the early 1990s, the Rev. Musemakweli found that he could not continue his studies and returned home. He helped rebuild the Theological Seminary in Rwanda after the war and is now back in Brussels in his final year of studies. When he finishes he will return to lead the new seminary.

In the next few pages you will catch a glimpse of the future through brief profiles of a few of our current scholars. I hope that you'll be as excited as we are to see how the church worldwide is continuing to plant the seeds for a new crop of bright and capable leaders for the ministry and mission of the world-wide church of the twenty-first century!

David L. Maxwell is Coordinator for the Office of Global Education and International Leadership Development, Worldwide Ministries Division, PC(USA).

Hope Antone

Hope Antone is a young woman with a mission. She has already made her mark as a leader in the United Christian Church of the Philippines, the Christian Conference of Asia, and the Asia/Pacific Region of the World Student Christian Federation. But Hope feels the need to do more and to be prepared for the challenge by pursuing graduate studies here in the United States. She says, "I believe that Christian mission is God's call to all Christians to carry out the will of God in the world by continuing the life-giving deeds of Jesus Christ. I take my cue from Jesus' statement, 'If you have faith in me, you will do the things I've been doing; you will do even greater things than these for I am going to the Father...' (John 14:12, author's trans.)."

Since she started her studies at the Presbyterian School of Christian Education (Union-PSCE) in Richmond, Virginia, Hope has seen the need to articulate a theory of religious education that takes into account the religious pluralism of Asia. "I just feel that religious diversity is a reality and that people in religious education can facilitate a better understanding among faith communities that tend to be in conflict," she says. Since coming to the United States, Hope has continued to pursue her interests in liberation theology, feminism, womanism, and ecological concerns as areas religious education needs to incorporate into its church and seminary programs. She participated in a study tour of Central America (comparing liberation theologies in Latin America and the Philippines), in the Presbyterian Women's Gathering in Louisville, Kentucky, and in a workshop on migration with the National Network of Presbyterian College Women.

Of her Union-PSCE experience, Hope says, "I am learning so many things. Theory and practice go together. Classical subjects can be taught in conversation with contemporary trends, as my theology course has done. As an international student I believe I have something to contribute to the learning environment both of the school and of the churches here in the United States. My professors have helped me share the gifts of my experiences and perspectives." Hope Sedillo Antone is in her third year of doctoral studies at Union-PSCE. After graduation she plans to return to her country and the Asian region.

Mary Basta

Mary Basta thought that the schools of the Synod of the Nile were not doing as good a job as they could. "Teachers, administrators, and others who work with children," she said, "had no training in how to work with students of different ages." So when Dr. Safwat El Biady, director of the synod schools, asked her to chair a committee to plan for a new school of education, she accepted with enthusiasm!

The result was the founding of the New Ramses College, of which she was chosen principal. "Now, after three years," she says, "we have twenty-one classes and an ongoing program of teacher training."

But, in order to maximize her own contribution to the new college, Mary decided to work on a masters degree in educational administration at the University of South Carolina (USC)—and the Office of Global Education of the Presbyterian Church (U.S.A.) decided to help. She is in her second year at USC in Columbia and plans to return to Cairo in August 1999 to resume her leadership of New Ramses College.

Mary Basta is a member of the Heliopolis Presbyterian Church of the Synod of the Nile. "What my church taught me," she says, "is that Christ lived his life for others, and that is what we are called to do."

She adds, "The hope of any country, developing or developed, is its children. They will fail us only if we fail them!"

Pat Baxter

Patricia May Baxter is a minister of the Presbytery of Cape Town of the Presbyterian Church of Southern Africa (PCSA) and is a doctoral candidate in theology at the Presbyterian School of Christian Education (PSCE) in Richmond, Virginia. As one of seven women pastors in the PCSA, Pat is keenly interested in feminist theology and women's issues, as well as in studies of human development and comparative spirituality.

But Pat is no cloistered intellectual. She is a woman who believes in putting her faith into action. As one of her professors said, "Pat's faith commitment has been tested—and deepened—in the struggle against apartheid in which she took a difficult, sometimes dangerous and unpopular public stand." Pat wants to live in a just society. She also wants to be part of a nurturing church. One of her interests is in African and Reformed spirituality.

Pat was once asked, "Why go to the United States to work on African spirituality?" Her answer was a ringing tribute to the value of study abroad, or at least of studying at PSCE! She said: "I delighted, blossomed, and grew in PSCE's learning environment. . . . Since my brief encounter with Dr. Izzie's [Dr. Isabel Rogers] classes in the history of Christian thought and her inspiring moderatorial tour of South Africa, I have longed to absorb and integrate her wisdom and 'dynamos' into my theology/praxis." We are sure that Pat Baxter will integrate Dr. Izzie's wisdom and 'dynamos'—and a great deal more—into her life and thought.

Asked what message she had for North American Christians, Pat replied, "I am grateful to the people who have offered me genuine hospitality. However, it is my concern that there is an ethos of self-sufficiency here—and blindness to the fact that other countries have much to offer. I grieve that the United States is considered a 'developed nation,' while others are considered 'developing.'"

And the challenge back home?

". . . to bring true racial integration among the people" and "to develop a viable Christian community that is a witness to peace and prosperity."

Geza Borbely

Geza Borbely was born in the little town of Fehergyarmat, Hungary, when that country was still under Communist rule. But by the time he was seventeen things had changed: "Since 1989," said Geza, "the Hungarian people have had the chance to live in a democratic society, which means that we can practice our religion freely!" That meant a lot to Geza Borbely. After high school he enrolled in the Reformed Theological Academy of Sarospatak where, he says, "I began to understand about God's marvelous work, became a Christian, and received a new life in Jesus Christ."

Geza plans to be a pastor in the Reformed Church of Hungary, helping his people recover and deepen their long and honored Reformation tradition. And like the sixteenth-century Reformers before him, Geza has an active and scholarly interest in the Old Testament. "From my first year in the theological seminary," he says, "I have been deeply interested in Old Testament and the Hebrew language."

Geza Borbely thinks that this is important for preaching.

So, to prepare for his career as a pastor and teacher, Geza applied to Louisville Presbyterian Theological Seminary in Kentucky and to the International Leadership Development (ILD) Scholarship Program of the Presbyterian Church (U.S.A.). He was accepted by both the seminary and the ILD program and is presently studying at Louisville Seminary.

When asked about his plans for the future, he responded (modestly), "I don't plan anything, but I would like to serve the Lord in that place where he leads me."

Asked what he sees as the most important challenge facing Christians in Hungary, he replied, "To live in that way of life that the

Geza, bottom left, with family.

people can recognize that we are Christians"—and then added, "Let your light shine before others, so that they may see your good works and give glory to your Father in heaven" (Matt. 5:16).

Saijai Chaiyasate

When Saijai Chaiyasate applied to the World Council of Churches for a scholarship to study dance she was told that "dance" does not fit the WCC criteria! She was referred to the Presbyterian Church (U.S.A.) Office of Global Education and International Leadership Development, which approved her application. Saijai is now studying at the California Institute of the Arts.

Why dance? What does dance have to do with the Christian life? Saijai thinks it has a lot to do with it. Says Saijai, "Dance is a gift from God."

Saijai loves to teach people how to dance and believes dance is a special way to communicate and help people express their thankfulness to God. Before winning her scholarship to study in California, Saijai was an instructor in Thai and modern dance in the communication arts department of Payap University in Chaing Mai, Thailand, a Christian university associated with the Church of Christ in Thailand.

Saijai is now recognized on both sides of the globe as a gifted teacher and an outstanding practitioner of her art. In her recommendation of Saijai for an ILD scholarship, the Rev. Prakai Nontawasee of the McGilvary Faculty of Theology at Payap said, "It is interesting to watch how fast she is learning the art of dancing and growing in her competence in both Thai and Western music. She is well loved by her students."

And Professor Cristyne Lawson, dean of the school of dance at Cal Arts, makes these observations, "Saijai is a beautiful dancer with an innate artistic expression. She possesses the rare quality of being in complete control and at the same time totally vulnerable and present. Ms. Chaiyasate also possesses a very sharp critical eye and is extremely perceptive in writing about what she sees. Her opinions are strong and clear. She is a welcome addition to the master's program and I look forward to her thesis concert."

Many people are looking forward to her return to Thailand, to her teaching career at Payap University, and to the excitement and delight she will contribute to the Church of Christ in Thailand.

Yoon-Jae Chang

Yoon-Jae Chang is a member of the Presbyterian Church of Korea (PCK) who is studying at Union Theological Seminary in New York. When asked "Why New York?" he replied, ". . . To stimulate fresh theological thinking and to experience the pluralism of New York." Yoon-Jae was born in Seoul, Korea, and was educated in mission schools. As a student at Yonsei University he was active in the Student Christian Movement. Then something happened. Yoon-Jae put it this way, "Scales fell from my eyes when my friend's mother, whom I loved very much, jumped from the balcony of her shabby apartment. She was in despair over her son's arrest by the military in December 1982. It was then that I began to see those sunken eyes and haggard faces of the poor Korean minjung.

"Some years later, taking political asylum in the Philippines and visiting many oppressed Asian communities, I found the same poor people suffering and struggling in the midst of hunger and massive poverty. I could not resist wrestling with a theological question: What has God to do with these oppressed people?"

Yoon-Jae has been struggling with this question ever since, taking his question with him as he has pursued his education and worked in the Christian Conference of Asia (CCA) and the National Council of Churches in Korea (NCCK). He is a member of the Galilee Presbyterian Church of Seoul and has not forsaken the church that gave him his faith. He plans to be active both in the PCK as well as with its educational and ecumenical ministries. Said the Rev. Sang-Hak Kim, general secretary of the PCK, in recommending Yoon-Jae for a scholarship to study at Union Theological Seminary in New York, "I have no doubt that Yoon-Jae Chang's study in the United States, particularly in the setting of Union, will offer him a fresh idea of theological thinking. This will be a gift to the PCK and the Korean churches, especially in the coming era when a more comprehensive and diverse approach to Christian social mission will be required."

Says Yoon-Jae, "I will return to work for the suffering and struggling people of Asia as a scholar, ecumenical activist, and pastor."

Luis Mariusso, Jr.

Born in the city of Campinas of nominally Catholic parents, Luis was not much interested in religion until his teenage years. Then his girl-friend, Marta, a member of a Catholic renewal group called "Renovaçao Carismática," gave him a Bible. Not long afterwards Luis went to work in a factory near Saõ Paulo, where he and his friends started a lunchtime Bible study. There he learned about "the sin condition of human beings and the great plan of salvation in Jesus Christ." Said Luis, "I found personally my Savior and accepted him in my life." He started to attend a Baptist church with his friends.

Soon Luis was deep into the work of the church, especially evangelism. "My principal interest," he says, "was the salvation of souls."

After four years in the Baptist seminary and training in mission work in Paraguay, Luis was called to the Independent Baptist Church in Fortaleza, Ceara, in the drought-stricken northeast of Brazil. There he met the Rev. Eriberto Soto, enrolled in the Theological Seminary of the Independent Presbyterian Church (IPI) of Brazil, and received a degree in religious science.

Having made his mark with Presbyterians, Luis was encouraged to come to the United States for a master's degree in theological stud-ies and return as coordinator of the Center for Missionary Training of the IPI in the Northeast.

With the help of a Leadership Development Grant from the Presbyterian Church (U.S.A.), Luis is in his second year at the Northern Baptist Seminary in Lombard, Illinois.

Luis Mariusso has come a long way from Campinas. Marta is still with him. She and Luis have been married now for more than ten years. They have two sons, Luis Filipe and Luis Matheus. All will soon return to Brazil to take up, once more, their lives among the Presbyterians!

Hector Méndez

Hector Méndez is a model for pastors working under difficult conditions. He grew up in a Roman Catholic family, but became interested in the Protestant church while attending a Presbyterian school near his home. As a youth he demonstrated his leadership ability, visiting every Presbyterian church in Cuba and preaching in many.

Then, in 1960, the situation in Cuba changed. The communist revolution hit and threw the churches into confusion. Said Méndez, "Many pastors and lay leaders abandoned the country . . . and the churches were left with few members." But Méndez decided to stay. "In this moment," he said, "I decided to enter seminary and to become a pastor in Cuba."

He began his studies at the Evangelical Theological Seminary in Matanzas in 1962 and in October 1965 was ordained. It was a difficult time to be a pastor in Cuba: pastors often had to work without transportation and other resources and to endure the incomprehension of the government. Many people in the churches also did not understand why their pastors preferred to stay in Cuba. But he would serve three or four churches at one time, and sometimes as many as eight. "During all those years," he said, "we had many opportunities to leave and work in other countries but always we rejected those invitations."

In recent years, however, the situation in Cuba has changed and the people have begun to overflow the congregations. Many young people are filling the churches and Matanzas Seminary has enrolled its biggest class yet.

Now that things are better, Hector Méndez has decided to complete his studies for the doctor of ministry degree. With support from the Presbyterian Church (U.S.A.) he is studying at the South Florida Center for Theological Studies in Miami, Florida. He is especially interested in liberation theology, having taken a course from Gustavo Gutiérrez at the Catholic University of Lima, Peru, in 1978. Hector Méndez has been given the 1998 E. H. Johnson Award from the Presbyterian Church of Canada for those on the "cutting edge of ministry."

Hector Méndez is living proof that no situation is too difficult to overcome, that the preaching of the Word can be accomplished under any circumstance.

Jonathan Mensah

Jonathan Mensah sees great changes taking place in his country—traditional communities are breaking up, whole families are migrating to the South, and young people are facing the temptations of drugs and many other social vices. "Quite recently," says Jonathan, "the Presbyterian Church of Ghana has created a desk for children's work in the church." This program is creating a need for more Christian education facilitators and counselors, but there is nowhere in Ghana for them to be trained. Jonathan Mensah is preparing to help meet that need. He received an International Leadership Development Grant from the Presbyterian Church (U.S.A.) in 1998 and is currently studying at the Louisville Presbyterian Theological Seminary in Kentucky.

Jonathan Mensah, a first-generation Christian, was born in a little town ten miles east of Accra. He joined the Nungua Zimmermann Memorial Presbyterian Church in 1972, graduated from Trinity College of the University of Ghana in 1984, and is now an ordained minister of the Presbyterian Church of Ghana.

Says Jonathan, "My vision for the ministry is to preach Christ and to help Christians grow into a mature faith. This demands that the Christian faith must truly speak to the people and meet their needs in whatever situation they may find themselves. I believe that an improvement in Christian education, pastoral care, and counseling can help realize this vision."

Asked what message he had for Christians in the United States, Mensah replied, "Christians in the United States should evaluate their concept of mission. Mission is no more a situation where missionaries travel to other countries to evangelize. Now it is a question of learning from each other."

Elisée Musemakweli

S ome spiritual journeys are beyond our comprehension. When Elisée Musemakweli went to study theology in Belgium, Rwanda was in the midst of a civil war. Then in 1994 came news of a massacre of incomprehensible proportions. The first word to reach Elisée was that his house had been plundered and that his mother, two brothers, and seven of his brothers' children had been killed. Said Elisée at the time, "In spite of our faith we do not understand the sense of the deaths of my mother, brothers, relatives, and many other fellow countrymen. It is so painful and cruel that we cannot comprehend it."

Elisée was then in the midst of writing a dissertation on the theology and preaching of theologian Paul Tillich, but with the unbelievable news from home (by then twenty members of his extended family had been killed) he could no longer continue his studies. On July 29, 1994, he wrote to Dr. Richard Rodman, associate for Global Education and International Leadership Development in Louisville, "I cannot hide from you the fact that this tragedy of the Rwanda people has not only afflicted me in my inmost life, but has also affected my academic work. Assiduity on the work has diminished. . . . My wife, Josephine, and I feel totally depressed and don't know what to do." It was then that the Rev. Andrew Karamaga, president of the Presbyterian Church of Rwanda, called Elisée home to help with the work of healing and reconstruction. Dr. Rodman agreed that Elisée needed time out from his studies and that the best cure for his depression was to go home and help others take control of their lives.

Elisée did a remarkable job and is now back in Belgium for the last year of his doctoral studies. Plans are that he will return to Rwanda in 1999 to teach at the Protestant Theological Faculty of Butare.

Epilogue: A Note of Celebration and an Invitation

Surely one cannot read these remarkable stories of courage, commitment, achievement, and faith without a feeling of humility, pride, and deep gratitude:

> To our partner churches for planting the seeds and nurturing the growth of these incredible leaders in their youth;

> To the visionaries of the Presbyterian Church from many program areas who took watering can in hand by offering grants to emerging leaders around the world in order to strengthen the ministry and mission of the worldwide church;

> To past and present staff of the International Leadership Development Program and to past and present area coordinators of the Worldwide Ministries Division;

> To past and present mission personnel who left monies for this program in their wills, so convinced were they that the number one priority in mission is the training of national leaders;

> To the Presbyterians throughout this land whose generous giving has made this creative program possible, and most of all

> To a loving and faithful God who provided the increase!

We Presbyterians have good reason to celebrate during this Year with Education. Lest we become too self-congratulatory, however, let us remember that the story of international leadership development is still being told. There are, as David Maxwell has said, 100 wonderful students studying during this current school year. Yet the funds are not sufficient for this essential task of watering.

You, the faithful Presbyterians who provide the leadership in local churches across this country, who give sacrificially to mission projects of all kinds, still have your hand on the faucet to the water. We invite each of you and your churches—as a way of continuing the celebration of this Year with Education, as an act of commitment to future leaders still in their childhood who will need this help to meet the crucial needs of ministry in every area of the world in the next century—to give to the Extra-Commitment Opportunity Account #132342, which is set up especially for this purpose. The seeds are awaiting the moisture that you can provide.

Write to us or e-mail us at *geild@pcusa.org* for more information or a brochure describing the program. A typical scholarship costs $8,000 a year. A contribution of $20 per month will pay for a student's books. A contribution of $109 per month will pay for a student's food for the year. Or, if you are considering leaving money with the PC(USA) upon your death, consider talking with the Presbyterian Foundation about leaving a portion of your estate to fund international leadership development.

We thank you for helping us to plant and water in the past fifty years, and we ask for your continuing help in the years to come. Will you pray with us that God continues to give the increase?

The Office of Global Education and
International Leadership Development
100 Witherspoon Street, Room 3220,
Louisville, Kentucky 40202-1396
Phone: 502-569-5641

Called to Dream, Called to Action

[This poem by Rubem Alves of Brazil, also one of our International Leadership Development Scholars, was published in the Study Texts for the 23rd General Council of the World Alliance of Reformed Churches, Debrecen, Hungary, August 8–20, 1997, for Section 11 "Justice for All Creation." Rubem was a member of the committee that prepared the study texts. The theme for the 23rd General Council was "Break the Chains of Injustice" from Isaiah 58:6. It seems a fitting way to close this book: by calling each one of us to continuing partnership with God in planting and watering the garden of international leadership—and to the eternal dream of living in communion with the "creative word of God."]

God as Father. God as Mother. God as Wind.
These are metaphors.
Attempts to put into words that which is beyond all words.

God as gardener. God plants a garden.
The universe is destined for Paradise—
joy, pleasure for God, for women and men, for all beings.
God destined us to be partners—
put tools in our hands, pruning hooks and ploughs;
put words in our mouth,
and invited us to name all created beings in the garden,
so that they may become our brothers and sisters.
Words—they are of two kinds.
Some are produced by the brain:
they serve as tools.
With them we build boats, bridges, wings.
These are the words of knowledge, science, and technology.
We cannot survive without them. They give us the means to life.
Alone they have no power to create happiness:
Boats, but not the vision of unseen lands;
Bridges, but not the vision of the garden beyond the abyss;
Wings, but not the vision of paradise to which we should fly.
They can break the chains of oppression,
but cannot provide the vision of freedom.
For vision, a different kind of word is needed.
A word which no brain can produce.
It comes with the wind. It is given to the heart. It is grace.

When the heart hears it, it begins to dream.
It is power to see beyond the visible.
Those who dream are those who provide direction
to boats, bridges, and wings.
They give reasons to our lives.
They are the prophets, the poets, the seers.
The words the community of the spirit is called to give,
these words are of a very special kind.
They have the colors of the rainbow,
the music of laughter and crying,
the perfume of flowers,
the hands of a lover,
the taste of bread and wine.

God speaks and life blossoms,
God's Spirit is constantly at work re-creating the world.
In Jesus, God dwells among us holding all things together
To live in communion with the creative word of God;
To say the words which re-create:
That is the mission of the community of faith.

Rubem Alves

Year with Education Hymn
(Fourth Stanza)

By Jane Parker Huber

Call forth to a global vision

Leaders faithful, strong and wise,

Worthy of a new day's mission,

Where the greatest needs arise.

May our knowledge lead to serving

All your people everywhere—

Goals established, faith unswerving,

Actions guided by our prayer.